WITTGENSTEIN

1889 - 1951

SUNY Series in Philosophy
George R. Lucas, Jr., Editor

SUNY Series in Logic and Language
John T. Kearns, Editor

WITTGENSTEIN

An Introduction

Joachim Schulte

Translated by
William H. Brenner and John F. Holley

State University of New York Press

Published by
State University of New York Press, Albany

For information, address State University of New York
Press, State University Plaza, Albany, N.Y. 12246

Production by Diane Ganeles
Marketing by Dana E. Yanulavich

Library of Congress Cataloging-in-Publication Data

Schulte, Joachim.
    [Wittgenstein. English]
    Wittgenstein : an introduction / Joachim Schulte : translated by
William H. Brenner and John F. Holley.
        p. cm.
    Translation of: Wittgenstein.
    Includes bibliographical references and index.
    ISBN 0-7914-1081-1 (alk. paper). — ISBN 0-7914-1082-X(pbk.:
alk. paper)
    1. Wittgenstein, Ludwig, 1889–1951.   I. Title.
B3376.W564S2913   1992
192—dc20   91-23522
                                                    CIP

10 9 8 7 6 5

Contents

Author's Preface

I want to introduce Wittgenstein to people who may have no previous acquaintance with his philosophy. The only things expected of the reader are general knowledge, good will, and readiness to read a sentence more than once; these often are more helpful than knowledge of technical philosophical terminology. Although I talk about Wittgenstein's career, distinctive traits, and achievements (as one always does when introducing someone), the main focus is his philosophy. I try to discuss most of Wittgenstein's central ideas, but without attempting "ideal completeness." And though always concerned to keep in view the aspect of gradual shifting and changing in his thought, I had to present it in a simplified and schematic way in order to preserve a clear overview. Ever since my first encounter with the *Tractatus* I have dealt with Wittgenstein again and again, devoting some years almost exclusively to him; and I have made my small contribution to the scholarly literature. This book is intended more for the student than for the scholar.

Secondary literature is mentioned in the few instances in which I extracted specific information from it. Other than that, I occasionally refer to passages en passant, in order to illustrate current controversies and striking misunderstandings. Of course, I still must acknowledge my gratitude to the Wittgenstein literature, for I remember only one book about Wittgenstein that taught me nothing—and that I never finished reading.

I profited from talks with teachers, friends, and the few Wittgenstein experts who are not teachers or friends or both, almost as much as from books. So, although they may have by now long forgotten it, I would like to thank those who provided me with material for one or more remarks in this book: Gordon Baker, John Baker, Deiter Birnbacher, Peter Hacker, Rudolf Haller, Brian McGuinness, Eva Picardi, Rush Rhees, and George Henrik von Wright.

Translators' Preface

This introduction provides a useful and interesting account of the various stages of Wittgenstein's thought. It is concise but not excessively compressed, substantive but not overloaded with developmental or technical detail, informed by the latest scholarship but not pedantic. Beginners will find it accessible and seasoned students of Wittgenstein will appreciate it for the illuminating overview it provides.

We are responsible for the translations of the Wittgenstein texts. We did, however, frequently consult—and learn from—the work of D. F. Pears, B. F. McGuinness, G. E. M. Anscombe, and others.

We want to thank Karin Hirt for helping us get this work underway and Mary K. Deegan for helpful stylistic suggestions throughout. We hope they will enjoy reading the final product.

1

***

Introduction

Life

Ludwig Wittgenstein, the youngest of eight children, was born in Vienna on April 26, 1889.[1] His parents—Karl and Leopoldine ("Poldy" née Kalmus)—possessed considerable wealth, which Karl had acquired as a businessman in the steel industry. Karl Wittgenstein was an impressive figure, and it was not only his business competitors who found him threatening. No one dared oppose his views.[2] His way of life was extravagant. It included a mansion in the city, a number of houses and parcels of land in the country, and the maintenance of the artists he admired—including Klimt and the Secessionists. He demanded that his sons subject themselves to his will and study to become "respectable" businessmen, engineers, or (best of all) both. The mother concerned herself with music, especially the piano, while the children were reared mostly by nannies, governesses, and private tutors. Karl Wittgenstein was of Jewish descent, Leopoldine partly so. But the family was completely assimilated. (Ludwig's final school diploma shows his best grade to be an "excellent" in Roman Catholic doctrine.) He attended a public school in Linz for just three years. Before that he had been privately tutored, but—as his father later discovered much to his chagrin—he learned in the process as little as his siblings had learned

---

1. Biographical sources are mentioned in the bibliography.

2. There is a collection of Karl Wittgenstein's newspaper articles and speeches. See bibliography.

before him. Early on he showed a talent for mechanical things, and as a child he built a tiny sewing machine that actually worked.

The first college Wittgenstein attended was the *Technische Hochschule* in Berlin-Charlottenburg, where he studied three semesters of engineering, and where he seemed to have enjoyed the musical scene. (He later reported that back in Berlin he went to see Wagner's *Die Meistersinger* thirty times.) After leaving Berlin he went to Manchester, England, where he worked very enthus- iastically on numerous technical projects at the university, without ever finishing one of them. Among other things, he participated in a series of kite-flying and weather-watch experiments and, towards the end of his stay in Manchester, was busy with the construction of an airplane propeller.

Through a remark in a document that was, by chance, preserved, we know that as early as 1909 Wittgenstein tried to solve Bertrand Russell's well-known "paradox," namely, the contradiction that arises from assuming the existence of a set of all sets that does not contain itself as an element.[3] His interest in problems of mathematical logic dates back at least to this point. But the official transfer to the study of logic and philosophy did not occur until he enrolled at Trinity College at the beginning of 1912, follow- ing a trial visit to Cambridge in 1911. The suggestion to study with Russell in Cambridge possibly came from Gottlob Frege, whom Wittgenstein had visited at his home in Jena in 1911. At that time, and for a long time after, Frege's *Fundamental Laws of Arithmetic* and Russell's *Principles of Mathematics* were Wittgenstein's favorite books. What- ever else he became acquainted with in philosophy he con- sidered confused, even when (as in the case of G. E. Moore, for example) he admired the author personally.[4] (He ap-

---

3. McGuinness, *Wittgenstein: A Life,* p. 81.

4. It is impossible to determine what Wittgenstein did *not* read. He himself talked about his reading only sporadically. And, although reports from friends and students allow us to determine authors with whom he was familiar and books he had read, reports on Wittgenstein's *lack* of knowledge have to be approached very carefully—especially since Wittgenstein enjoyed

pears to have read hardly any philosophy except for Schopenhauer.[5])

With Russell, to whom Wittgenstein introduced himself as a prospective "pilot" or "aeronaut," there began a warm (but for Russell, often distressing) friendship.[6] Wittgenstein sought out the older man daily, discussing logical or philosophical problems with him for hours, refusing to be disturbed even when Russell had visitors or needed to change for dinner. Russell thought highly of him, soon recognizing his genius; and when his sister Hermine (Mining) visited, he frankly told her: "We expect the next big step in philosophy to be taken by your brother."[7]

Wittgenstein developed a close friendship with David Pinsent, a younger man who finished studies in mathematics before deciding to study law. (The *Tractatus* is dedicated to him.) In 1912 Wittgenstein and Pinsent went on vacation to Iceland and in 1913 to Norway. During this time in Cambridge, he came to know a number of people, including G. E. Moore and John Maynard Keynes, who were to become very important for him—people who often later provided advice or help. The trip to Norway was important because it was there that Wittgenstein decided to seclude himself in order to continue his logical studies in peace and quiet. After dictating parts of his first writings ("Notes on Logic") in Russell's presence at the end of 1913,

---

emphasizing, perhaps exaggerating, his lack of extensive book learning. See Drury, "Conversations with Wittgenstein," p. 171, and Mays, "Recollections of Wittgenstein," p. 84. What we can say, in light of the existing reports, is that Wittgenstein's approach to the authors he did read was not that of a scholar. He was not interested in completeness. But he experienced with great intensity whatever he did read or hear about and kept coming back to it.

5. See his first extant letter to Russell (probably June 1912).

6. In his autobiography and in other writings, Russell describes his relationship with Wittgenstein (a relationship that was later to cool down considerably). More reliable than these descriptions are Russell's letters to Lady Ottoline Morrell, which are quoted in detail in McGuinness, *Wittgenstein: A Life;* and Clark, *The Life of Bertrand Russell.*

7. Hermine Wittgenstein, "My Brother Ludwig," p. 3.

Wittgenstein left Cambridge and moved to Norway where Moore visited him in April. Subsequently they quarreled over an examination formality and, as a result, it was fifteen years before they spoke to each other again.

In Norway, Wittgenstein probably wrote parts of the notes which later provided the basis for the work on the *Tractatus*. While staying in Austria in the summer of 1914, he hastened to donate part of the wealth he had inherited from his father in 1913 to needy artists.[8] For advice on the distribution of the sum of 100,000 kroners, he contacted Ludwig von Ficker, editor of a periodical much admired by the famous Austrian social critic Karl Kraus called *Der Brenner*. In this way, Rilke, Trakl, Else Lasker-Schüler, and Oscar Kokoschka obtained support from Wittgenstein. War was declared right after that, and, in spite of a double hernia, Wittgenstein volunteered to serve and was accepted.

What Wittgenstein liked least about war was his fellow soldiers. He showed great bravery, was decorated a number of times, and had reached the rank of lieutenant by the time he was taken prisoner, just before the armistice. The war's effect on him can be seen when comparing photographs taken before the war with those taken later. Amazingly often he was able to work on his book in spite of the adverse conditions. Three manuscripts that were preserved from this time represent a considerable part of the preliminary work for his book, which was finished during his last leave from the front (July to September 1918). The book, *Logisch-philosophische Abhandlung* (Logical-Philosophical Treatise) is better known by the title inspired by Moore and later given to the English edition, namely, the *Tractatus Logico-Philosophicus*.

While attending officer's school in Olmütz, Wittgenstein met a circle of young people with whom he stayed in contact for a long time. The main friendship he developed

---

8. Characteristic of Wittgenstein's attitude towards death is a letter to Russell written on January 21, 1913: "Yesterday afternoon my father died. He had the nicest death I can imagine; he fell asleep like a child without any pain. During the last hours I was not sad for a moment, but full of joy. I believe that this death was worth an entire life."

there was with an interior designer and student of Adolph Loos, Paul Englemann. (Englemann was to write exceptionally penetrating recollections of Wittgenstein's personality and historical circumstances.) Wittgenstein's sister Mining writes in her notes that "already back then there were signs in Ludwig of the profound transformation that was to come to fruition only after the war . . . . The other soldiers called him 'the man with the Gospel' because he always carried Tolstoy's adaptation of the Gospels with him."

In the summer of the last war year, Wittgenstein learned that his friend David Pinsent had died in an accident. Maybe it was because of this that he wanted to commit suicide at this time, but his Uncle Paul convinced him to work on his book instead—for which Wittgenstein thanked him in the first draft of the *Tractatus*.[9] Suicidal thoughts tormented Wittgenstein again and again, and three of his four brothers did commit suicide.[10]

Wittgenstein spent ten months as a prisoner of war in Italy, where he got to know the teacher Ludwig Hänsel and the sculptor Michael Drobil. Upon his release in August 1919, he returned to Vienna. He made it very clear to his family that he wanted to start a new life: He gave his

---

9. *Prototractatus,* p. 2.

10. On the theme of suicide, two testimonies are to be considered: (1) *Notebooks,* 1/10/1917:

> If suicide is allowed, then everything is allowed.
>   If anything is not allowed, then suicide is not allowed.
>   This throws light on the nature of ethics. For suicide is, so to speak, the elementary sin.
>   And when one investigates it, it is like investigating mercury vapor in order to comprehend the nature of vapors.
>   Or is even suicide in itself neither good nor evil!

Compare Schopenhauer's thoughts about suicide, which Wittgenstein certainly knew.

(2) Letter to Englemann dated 6/21/1920:

> I know that suicide is always a dirty business. For there's no way at all that one *can* will one's own annihilation, and everyone who

fortune to his brothers and sisters (his only possession was the cottage he had built in 1914 in Norway, and even that he tried to give away a few times). Then he registered and enrolled at the teacher training school in Vienna's "Third District," close to which he later built the house for his sister Gretl Stonborough, which has been restored. In 1920, after one year of studies, and after he had worked for a while as a gardener's assistant in the monastery at Neuberg, he became a grammar school teacher and began his work in Lower Austria, near Kirchberg am Wechsel.

He remained a grammar school teacher until 1926.[11] Because he took his responsibilities seriously, he was, time and again, at odds with the parents of his pupils and often depressed. Apparently he had prescribed this work for himself as a kind of medicine that was to enable him to lead a "decent" life. ("Decent" was a word that Wittgenstein used again and again with special emphasis. In this situation he no doubt wanted most of all to be engaged in selfless activity and work himself to exhaustion, creating a prophylaxis against the "vanity" which he feared.) He describes his activities in characteristic language in a letter to Keynes dated October 18, 1925:

> I have resolved to remain a teacher as long as I feel that the difficulties I am experiencing might be doing me some good. When you have a toothache, the pain from the toothache is reduced by putting a hot water bottle to your face. But that works only as long as the heat hurts your face. I will throw away the bottle as soon as I notice that it no longer provides that special pain that does my character good.

---

has ever imagined what's involved in suicide, knows that suicide is always a *taking oneself by surprise*. But nothing is worse than being compelled to take oneself by surprise.

Cf. McGuinness, *Wittgenstein: A Life*, p. 157.

11. Concerning this period, see Wünsche's study, *Der Volksschullehrer Ludwig Wittgenstein*. This volume contains a number of interesting documents, for example the letters of Wittgenstein (and his sister Mining) to Ludwig Hänsel.

A letter written two years later included the laconic footnote: "I could no longer stand the hot water bottle."

Wittgenstein's first and only philosophical book published during his lifetime appeared while he was serving as an elementary school teacher. Without success, he had tried several times to interest various publishers—first of all, and significantly, the publishers of Karl Kraus and Otto Weininger—in his *Logical-Philosophical Treatise*. He met with Russell again at the end of 1919, in Amsterdam, for lengthy discussions of that treatise. When Russell offered to help by contributing a foreword, Wittgenstein felt that he had no choice but to tell his friend clearly that he did not want to have his book appear with that foreword (cf. letter of May 6, 1920). In the end, he gave up his own efforts to get it published and turned matters over to Russell and Russell's friends. Consequently, first publication was in Wilhelm Osterwald's *Annalen der Naturphilosophie* (1921); a year later it was published in England as a dual-language book.

The question as to who actually translated the book into English has not been completely settled. The young Frank Ramsey, a very gifted mathematician from Cambridge with whom Wittgenstein was corresponding at the time, had an important part in this work. Ramsey visited Wittgenstein while the latter was a schoolteacher in Lower Austria and had conversations with him that he subsequently reported to Keynes. It was through the help of these two friends that Wittgenstein again visited England in the summer of 1925 after an absence of eleven years, an event which occasioned the remark in the letter to Keynes already quoted, to the effect that if he were to give up school teaching, he probably would look for a position in England.

But things did not happen quite that quickly. After quitting the teaching profession, he busied himself with the construction of a house for his sister—work that fascinated and absorbed him. Superficially showing the influence of Loos, in many ways the building reflects Wittgenstein's own personality: there is a sober matter-of-factness combined with the solemn upward thrust of a cathedral, a painstaking exactness in the completion of each detail, and a total lack of concern for the comfort of the person living there.

By the end of 1928 this work too was finished. The time for return had come—for return to philosophy, to Cambridge, and to a freer way of life. But there is a story even behind this change, which seemed to come about so quickly. The members of the Vienna Circle, who were so interested in philosophy, mathematics, and science and who were so important for the development of analytical philosophy and philosophy of science, already had attempted to make contact with Wittgenstein by the mid '20s, at first with no success at all. It was not until two or three years later, while Wittgenstein was still busy building the house for his sister, that a meeting between Moritz Schlick and Wittgenstein became possible. Later on there were conversations with Waismann, Carnap, Feigl, and the woman Feigl later was to marry. However, Wittgenstein often refused to talk about philosophy and enjoyed reading poetry aloud while turning his back on the respectful, but confused, scientists.[12]

Philosophical discussions eventually evolved with Schlick and his assistant Friedrich Waismann. Waismann kept notes on many of these discussions and collaborated on a book project with Wittgenstein into the early 1930s.[13] Through this association with some of the members of the Vienna Circle, Wittgenstein came into contact with new thinking in the philosophy of mathematics, especially with the ideas of the intuitionist Brouwer. (He no doubt already had heard some of these ideas from Ramsey.) When

---

12. Cf. Mrs. Schlick's recollection of her husband's first visit with Wittgenstein: "Again . . . I observed with interest the reverential attitude of the pilgrim. He returned in an ecstatic state, saying little, and I felt I should not ask questions." Quoted in the editor's forward to *WVC*, p. 14.

13. Announced repeatedly since 1930 in advertisements for the writings of the Vienna Circle, the book finally appeared in 1976 as Waismann's *Logik, Sprache, Philosophie*. It is among the most important sources of information on Wittgenstein's thinking during the early thirties. [The English version appeared in 1965, under the title *The Principles of Linguistic Philosophy*.]

Wittgenstein attended a lecture by Brouwer in Vienna in the spring of 1928, his interest was awakened. This was possibly the first, or the decisive, step towards his return to philosophy.

In early 1929 Wittgenstein arrived in Cambridge. He was a "research student" until June, when, on the merits of the *Tractatus,* he received a doctorate. His old friends—Russell, Keynes, Ramsey, and Moore—spoke in his behalf. At first he received a stipend, but shortly after completing the doctorate, was awarded a fellowship at Trinity College—a temporary appointment, but one which he held until 1936. In no time his lectures became much talked about. In addition to class notes and elaborations, several descriptions of Wittgenstein's lectures graphically depict his pedagogical procedures. Norman Malcolm describes them as follows:

> It is hardly correct to speak of these meetings as "lectures," although this is what Wittgenstein called them. For one thing, he was carrying on original research in these meetings. He was thinking about certain problems in a way that he could have done had he been alone. For another thing, the meetings were largely conversation. Wittgenstein commonly directed questions to various persons present and reacted to their replies. Often the meetings consisted mainly of dialogue. Sometimes, however, when he was trying to draw a thought out of himself, he would prohibit, with a peremptory motion of the hand, any questions or remarks. There were frequent and prolonged periods of silence, with only an occasional mutter from Wittgenstein, and the stillest attention from the others. During these silences, Wittgenstein was extremely tense and active. His gaze was concentrated; his face was alive; his hands made arresting movements; his expression was stern.[14]

During these years Wittgenstein became a legendary figure. He showed a touching and, in the opinion of some of

---

14. Malcolm, *Memoir,* p. 25. Compare with the introduction of *WLL,* and the editor's preface to *WLA.* See further the description of D. A. T. Gasking and A. C. Jackson in Fann, ed., *Ludwig Wittgenstein: The Man and His Philosophy,* pp. 49–55.

his contemporaries, much too tyrannical concern for his students. His influence on them was enormous. Fania Pascal, Wittgenstein's Russian teacher, reported in her memoirs that she saw people in the 1960s whom she had never seen before and could tell at once that they had been influenced by Wittgenstein, for they had adopted expressions and mannerisms of speech that could have come only from him.[15]

Immediately after his return, Wittgenstein began to write. The conversations he had with Ramsey until the latter's early death in 1930 probably had a great influence on his themes and method.[16] Almost daily he made notes, made changes, dictated, had copies made, and then formulated everything all over again. In this way a lot of very comprehensive, typed manuscripts were produced in rapid succession, which Wittgenstein at first attempted to rework, but then neglected because his thoughts were moving in a different direction. Several works were dictated to students and then reproduced in very small editions. The *Blue Book* and the *Brown Book* circulated in this manner for many years before they finally were published in book form in 1958.

In 1935 Wittgenstein traveled for several weeks in the Soviet Union. He originally had planned to go with his friend and former student Francis Skinner, but an illness prevented Skinner from making the trip. For some time Wittgenstein had taken private lessons in Russian and apparently was a very talented student. There are some notes in Russian among his papers. Earlier he had shown a strong attraction to Russia, not only with regard to the works of its great writers, Tolstoy and Dostoyevski, but also with regard to several typical characteristics that he associated with the Russian people, their habits, and their customs. At the time he obviously wanted to determine

---

15. Pascal, "Wittgenstein: A Personal Memoir," p. 37.

16. Cf. preface to *PI*: "I was helped to realize these mistakes—in a measure that I myself am hardly able to estimate—by the criticism which my ideas encountered from Frank Ramsey, with whom I discussed them in countless conversations during the last two years of his life."

whether he might want to move there and take up a profession. Although the thought of Russia as a spiritual refuge is mentioned in his last letter to Engelmann, dated June 21, 1937,[17] Fania Pascal probably was correct in her impression that almost immediately after visiting Russia, Wittgenstein decided not to settle there.

The year 1936 was a turning point for Wittgenstein. The position at Trinity College expired, and the contract could not be extended. He decided to travel to Norway in order to work there again in solitude. In fact, he remained there, with only a few short interruptions, until the end of 1937 and wrote parts of what we have come to know as the *Philosophical Investigations* and the *Remarks On the Foundations of Mathematics.* Concentrating on the presentation of his ideas, which he had only gradually modified in the earlier writings of the 1930s, he was led in the end to reformulate them radically. In 1938 Wittgenstein returned to Cambridge. Because of the annexation of Austria to the German *Reich*, he had to decide whether to become a German citizen or to apply for British citizenship. As he wrote to Keynes on March 18, 1938, the idea of becoming an "imitation Englishman" had never appealed to him; however, the thought of becoming a German citizen was, aside from the abominable consequences, just "DREADFUL."[18] Thus, he became a British subject.

As a member of the Cambridge faculty, Wittgenstein held classes and applied for Moore's chair when it became vacant. For this purpose he and his student and friend Rush Rhees translated the existing part of the *Philosophical Investigations,* sending it to Keynes, who had a voice in the appointment procedure. Wittgenstein was offered the

---

17. Pascal, "Wittgenstein: A Personal Memoir," p. 44; cf. Rhees, ed., "Postscript," pp. 219ff.

18. This does not, of course, mean that Wittgenstein harbored anti-German sentiments. On the contrary, he regarded himself as belonging to the German cultural sphere and seems to have taken more from the Germans than from the Austrians in technical and military matters. For understandable reasons, however, he felt no sympathy for the German regime then in power.

position in the beginning of February 1939, and when he heard that his colleague and intellectual adversary C. D. Broad had expressed the opinion that "to deny Wittgenstein the chair would be the same as denying Einstein the chair in physics," he was very moved.[19] He wrote to Keynes, "Well now I *hope* that I will be a decent professor."

Officially Wittgenstein was a professor for about eight years after that; however, in reality he occupied the position only sporadically, for right after the outbreak of the war he enlisted in various support services. At first he worked in Guy's Hospital in London; later he worked in Newcastle with a physiological research group. In 1944 he retreated to Swansea, where he continued the work on the *Philosophical Investigations* in relative solitude. (The preface, which of course relates only to the [not yet completed] Part I, is dated "Cambridge, January, 1945.") Even during the war he repeatedly returned to Cambridge to hold occasional seminars; however, it was not until toward the end of 1944 that he once again resumed actual teaching responsibilities.

In the first half of 1947, Wittgenstein came to feel that he was no longer able to combine teaching with writing. In a letter to Moore dated February 18, 1947, he asks "whether it really did make sense to husband his strength in order to be able to teach people, most of whom were not able to learn anything." On the 27th of August he wrote to Malcolm, "I really would like to be some place by myself and attempt to write and at least get one part of my book ready for publication. I will never be able to do that as long as I am teaching here in Cambridge. I also feel that, aside and apart from writing, I need to catch my breath and to be alone to think without having to speak to anyone." Then the decision was made. Wittgenstein resigned his position and was released from duties in the last trimester of 1947. Visibly relieved, he wrote to Malcolm on the 16th of November:

---

19. Drury, "Conversations with Wittgenstein," p. 156.

... I shall cease to be professor on December 31st at 12 p.m. *Whatever* happens to me (& I am not at all sanguine about my future), I feel I did the only natural thing.

Following the war, Wittgenstein worked mainly on topics in philosophy of psychology. He continued to work on them in the following year and a half, a period he spent partly in Dublin and partly in various remote places in Ireland. Occasionally he interrupted these sojourns in order to travel to Cambridge or Vienna. The so-called Part II of *Philosophical Investigations* was for a long time the only testimony to the work of those years. The *Remarks on the Philosophy of Psychology* and *Last Writings on the Philosophy of Psychology,* which have appeared in the meantime, provide additional information on the direction of his thought during that time.

In July of 1949 Wittgenstein traveled to North America in order to visit his friend and former student Norman Malcolm.[20] He remained until October but in the meantime had become seriously ill. A medical examination, however, revealed no cause for concern. It was only after his return to England that prostate cancer was diagnosed. Wittgenstein traveled twice to Vienna and even to Norway toward the end of 1950. He lived either with Georg Henrik von Wright, his successor to the chair at Cambridge, with his former student Elizabeth Anscombe in Oxford, or in the London apartment of Rush Rhees. Often he was unable to work, perhaps because of the treatment with hormones and radiation. Occasionally, however, and particularly during the last months of his life, he wrote down thoughts that, as von Wright correctly says, "are the equal to the best he produced."[21]

Wittgenstein did not want to die in the hospital and was glad when his Cambridge physician, Dr. Bevan, offered to let him live in his house during the last weeks. He

---

20. Malcolm's well-known account of this stay is now supplemented by O. K. Bouwsma's *Wittgenstein: Conversations 1949–1951.*

21. von Wright, *Wittgenstein,* p. 31.

stayed there beginning in February 1951, continuing to write notes on the topic of certainty and visiting friends for light-hearted conversation. (On April 21 he visited the ailing von Wright, assuring him that it was not he himself but his astral body who was paying the call.) He died on April 29, 1951. Mrs. Bevan, who stayed up with him that night, reported that his last words were, "Tell them that I had a wonderful life." Some, remembering Wittgenstein's severity, tortured intensity, and often acerbic criticism were amazed when they heard that. Perhaps they would have been less amazed had they given more thought to the man's accomplishments.

Personality

"I find it impossible to say even a single word in my book about all that music has meant for me in my life. So how can I hope that anyone will understand me?"[22] In this remark, from a 1949 conversation, Wittgenstein is referring to the *Philosophical Investigations,* which was then in manuscript form. An important part in his life, music was a determining factor in the way Wittgenstein interacted with many of his friends and acquaintances.

Although he came from a very musical family and grew up in a house where Brahms and many other celebrities of the Vienna music world felt at home, for the longest time Wittgenstein himself played no instrument. As a youth he took piano lessons for a short time, but learned nothing. Music, especially the piano, was the most important thing in his mother's life, and his father played the violin. His eldest brother, the first to commit suicide, was a musical prodigy; Paul Wittgenstein, who was only little older, became a concert pianist. Paul lost an arm in the war, but stayed with his profession, playing with his left hand and commissioning compositions that he played in public. Ravel, for example, composed his piano concerto for the left hand for him. Ludwig cared little for these performances, which

---

22. Drury, "Conversations with Wittgenstein," p. 160.

he compared to circus acts, nor did he care for Paul's musical style. On the other hand, he had great respect for the performances and (apparently) the compositions of the blind organist, Labor, who enjoyed a special status in the Wittgenstein household.

Wittgenstein's own musical talent was expressed mostly in his ability to explain music and show how it should be played, and in a phenomenal talent for whistling, remarked on by those who knew him. He repeatedly demonstrated his critical, analytical ability to explain music. When professional musicians failed to take him seriously, he explained a piece of music until it was clear to them (much to their embarrassment) how much they had not understood of it, whereupon they enthusiastically begged him to explain everything. He regularly practiced his gift for whistling with many of his serious musician friends—for example by learning Schubert *lieder* with them and interpreting the vocal part through his whistling. When he became a teacher, he had to learn an instrument, and he decided on the clarinet. His sister Mining remarked, "I believe that was the beginning of his strong feeling for music. At any rate, he played with great musical sensitivity and found much pleasure in that instrument. Instead of keeping it in a case, he customarily carried it around in an old sock. . . ."[23]

In countless conversations about music, often after concerts or after listening to records at the house of a student or friend, Wittgenstein revealed time and again how intensely he listened and the extent of his ability to recognize musical connections. It was characteristic of him that breadth of knowledge was never important to him; what he wanted was in-depth penetration and understanding down to the smallest detail of whatever it was that occupied him at the moment. This was his customary approach to everything. He read his favorite books over and over

---

23. Hermine Wittgenstein, "My Brother Ludwig," p. 9. In a letter there is talk about his playing the clarinet part in Schubert's "The Shepherd on the Rock." This is the only concrete indication I have been able to find on Wittgenstein's abilities as a clarinetist.

again and always with the greatest attention to detail. He once advised a friend to pick out only one picture in a museum, take his time studying it, and then leave.

Musically—as in many other things—Wittgenstein was a man of the nineteenth century, especially the first half of the nineteenth century. Although Beethoven, Schubert, and Schumann were perhaps preeminent for him, other musical figures sometimes preoccupied him, depending probably on what concerned him most intensely at the time. Thus there was a period when he wanted to hear only Bach, and one when Brahms was especially important to him. And, as already mentioned, he claimed that during his time in Berlin he attended thirty performances of *Die Meistersinger.*

Among Wittgenstein's scattered written statements on music, most of them collected in the *Culture and Value,* a few are revealing about Wittgenstein himself. For example, there is a series of comments on Mendelssohn, for whom Wittgenstein felt a certain affinity (no doubt, in part, because he was Jewish): "Mendelssohn is not a peak, but rather a plateau. His Englishness. . . . Mendelssohn is like a person who is jolly only when everything is amusing anyway, or good when everyone around him is good; not really at all like a tree that stands fast no matter what is going on around it. I myself am like that too and am inclined to be that way" (1929, *CV,* p. 2). The comparison with Brahms is, therefore, also interesting because Brahms represents something that, in Wittgenstein's opinion, he himself lacked but which he would have liked to have had:

> There is definitely a certain relationship between Brahms and Mendelssohn, but I am not referring to the parts of Brahms's works reminiscent of Mendelssohn. What I have in mind could be expressed by saying: "Brahms does with perfect discipline what Mendelssohn did halfheartedly" or "Brahms is often perfected Mendelssohn." (1931, *CV,* p. 21).

Jewishness was an important theme for Wittgenstein, although precise statements in this regard are difficult to make on the basis of available evidence. Like Otto

Weininger, whom he admired, Wittgenstein tended (but less crassly) to attribute weak or feminine (though not necessarily negative) characteristics to what he considered Jewish. That sentiment is expressed in his notebooks primarily when he speaks of originality and reproduction, as in the following—a passage in which he also mentions the authors he felt had influenced his thinking.

> The Jewish "genius" can only be a saint. The greatest Jewish thinker is just talented. (Like me, for example.)
>
> There is, I believe, some truth in the thought that in my thinking I am merely reproductive. I do not believe that I have ever come up with a new way of thinking; on the contrary, it was always given to me by someone else. I only seized it passionately and applied it to my elucidations. I have been influenced in this way by Boltzmann, Hertz, Schopenhauer, Frege, Russell, Kraus, Loos, Weininger, Spengler, Sraffa. Can one add Breuer and Freud as examples of Jewish reproductivity?—What I come up with are new *metaphors.* (1931, *CV,* pp. 18–19).

Eight or nine years later he describes these circumstances in a similar manner and comes back to the comparison with Breuer and Freud:

> My originality (if that is the right word) is, I believe, an originality of the soil, not the seed. (Perhaps I do not have any seed of my own.) Cast the seeds onto my soil, and they will grow differently than on any other.
>
> Freud's originality was of this type too, I believe. I have always thought—without really knowing why—that the true seed of psychoanalysis came from Breuer, not from Freud. The seed grains from Breuer can only have been very small. *Courage* is always original. (1939/40, *CV,* p. 36).

Such statements must always be interpreted very carefully, for we do not know what the external and internal conditions were in Wittgenstein's life when he wrote them. In any case, he had a high regard for Freud as well as for himself, but he always saw the danger of vanity and the possibility that his thoughts—like Freud's—could become fashionable and trivialized into mere jargon. The fear that a fate similar to that of Freud's could befall his work was certainly one reason he did not publish his later writings.

The music of the nineteenth century was a natural part of Wittgenstein's life, and the same can be said of the literature of that period. Goethe is for Wittgenstein in many ways the "given and the accepted" model, the highest realization of what literature can be. Not given to quotation, Wittgenstein was fond of quoting Goethe, and the thought processes of the two have a certain similarity.

The great Russians, Tolstoy and Dostoyevski, played a special role. Again and again, Wittgenstein recommended Tolstoy's folk tales and Dostoyevski's *Brothers Karamasov* to his friends. However, he did not like everything of Tolstoy's—as is revealed in the following passage from a letter to Malcolm dated September 20, 1945—a passage that tells us something about his aesthetic ideals:

> I once tried to read *The Resurrection* but couldn't. You see, when Tolstoy simply tells a story, he impresses me infinitely more than when he addresses the reader. When he turns his back on the reader, then he seems to me *most* impressive. . . . His philosophy seems to me completely true when *hidden* in the story.

The impression of Wittgenstein expressed by Fania Pascal in her memoir is surely correct:

> To my mind, his feeling for Russia had more to do with Tolstoy's moral teaching, with Dostoyevski's spiritual insights, than with any political or social matters. He would view the latter, which certainly were not indifferent to him, in terms of the former.[24]

Wittgenstein also knew a few English authors, probably Dickens best of all. And, once he learned Norwegian, he read Ibsen and Bjørnson. His preference was, however, for Mörike and Keller, and he always had a weakness for Austrians like Grillparzer and Lenau, Nestroy and Kraus:

---

24. Pascal, "Wittgenstein: A Personal Memoir," p. 57.

I think that good Austrian work (Grillparzer, Leanu, Bruckner, Labor) is especially difficult to understand. It is in a certain sense more *subtle* than anything else, and its truth is never on the side of probability. (1929, *CV,* p. 3).

One should not overlook the fact that the motto of the *Philosophical Investigations,* as of the *Tractatus,* came from Austrian authors. The saying, "Progress characteristically appears greater than it really is," is from Nestroy's play, *The Protege,* while the quotation, ". . . and everything one knows, as opposed to having heard as just so much noise, can be stated in three words," is from *Literary Matters of the Heart* by Ferdinand Kürnberger (a passage, by the way, also quoted by Karl Kraus[25]).

Even mottos long considered but not selected are of interest here. The following lines are to be found among these unused quotations:

See the moon above?—
Only half of it can be seen
And yet it is full and round!

by Matthias Claudius, and

Nature has neither core
Nor husk,
It is all one.
Test yourself relentlessly,
To see if you are a core or a husk.

by Goethe. Gordon Baker and Peter Hacker correctly point out in their commentary that these and some of the other quotations considered for mottos play on the contrasts of exterior and interior, visible and invisible, reality and appearance.

[handwritten margin note: REALITY & APPEARANCE]

In addition to the various mottos, Wittgenstein's prefaces and drafts of prefaces reveal his view of his work and the world. The preface to the *Tractatus* will be discussed later, in Chapter 2. Here we shall discuss what is perhaps

---

25. Cf. McGuinness, *Wittgenstein: A Life,* p. 251.

the most straightforward record of his personal viewpoint, namely the brief (barely a half page long) foreword to the *Philosophical Remarks* of 1930. The first paragraph is as follows:

> This book is written for those who can appreciate its spirit. This is a spirit different from that of the main current of the European and American civilization of which we all are part. *This latter* (second) spirit expresses itself through progress, through the construction of forms that are ever larger and ever more complicated; the other (first-mentioned spirit), in a striving for clarity and perspicuity in whatever structure. The second spirit attempts to understand the world from the periphery, in its multifaceted appearance; the first, in its center or essence. So the second spirit strings together one formation with another, ascending, as it were, from step to step ever higher, while the other remains where it is, always attempting to comprehend the same thing.

Here again, as in the motto for the *Philosophical Investigations,* Wittgenstein takes issue with an optimistic faith in progress. Employing striking combinations in an earlier draft, he speaks of the "spirit of this civilization whose expression is the industry, architecture, music, fascism, and socialism of our time." He sees himself on the side of those who want to understand the essence of things, and it is interesting that he does not associate this quest for the essence with the image of ascending through stages, employing this image rather to characterize the quest for progress. The view that those seeking the essence are ever looking for the same thing is a view that (more in tenor than content) anticipates ideas in the *Philosophical Investigations,* for example, the idea that philosophy leaves everything the way it is (*PI,* § 124). The idea of a "striving for clarity and perspicuity, no matter what the structure" is perhaps the most striking thing in the quoted paragraph.

Interestingly enough, there always have been those who see in Wittgenstein a kind of positivist, or even a thinker driven by a delusion of scientific exactness to interpret everything in mathematical and technical formulas. But only someone who had never read a line of Wittgenstein could come up with such views. At the opposite extreme are those who attempt to correct such misapprehensions by unnecessarily emphasizing anything in Wittgenstein that is gloomy, partially formulated, intellectually pessimistic, and resistant to change. Although all of these characteristics are indeed present in Wittgenstein's work and in his personality, one should not infer that he is *against* clarity, knowledge, expression, or change. On the contrary, the quest for clarity is the very motor that drives *CLARITY* Wittgenstein's thinking. He just does not believe that the path to clarity is simple. He thought that the path, though difficult to find, is one that must be traversed—with all its detours and hindrances—by everyone striving for clarity. This is another aspect of Wittgenstein's "constructivist" ideas: one has to know how something is *put together* before one can talk about it. We cannot assume another's burden of practical learning; at best, we can help him with it. Taking on theoretical questions as if they were practical is one of the tricks of Wittgenstein's thinking. Often as a result of this procedure, not much of the question remains. But the process was worthwhile: "Although the question as to the essence may not be answered, once these painful contradictions have been removed, the intellect is no longer tormented and stops asking what has become an unjustified question."[26]

The second paragraph of the foreword to the *Philosophical Remarks* is more personal in its formulation but no less characteristic than the first:

> I would like to say "This book was written to the honor of God," but to say that today would just be chicanery, i.e., it would be misunderstood. It means the book is written in good will, and to the extent that it might be found to be written not with good will but rather out of vanity, etc., to that extent the author would wish to see it rejected. He

---

26. This quotation from Heinrich Hertz's *Principles of Mechanics* was to have served originally as the motto of the *Philosophical Investigations*. Quoted in Baker and Hacker, *Understanding and Meaning*, p. 16.

cannot make his book any less tainted by such faults than he is himself.

The work can only be as pure—that is, free from faults like vanity—as the author was successful in freeing himself from such wrong attitudes during and through the work. In this regard doing philosophy has a practical side: it is a kind of therapy that can free and satisfy us. Thus Wittgenstein's frequent employment of medical images:

> The philosopher treats a question; like an illness. (*PI*, § 255).

> One main cause of philosophical sickness—a one-sided diet: feeding one's thinking with only one kind of example. (*PI*, § 593).

But it is not just individuals—confused philosophers and scientists with their one-sided thinking and one-track minds—who are sick. The times are sick—the times in which one may no longer speak of a work written "to the honor of God," as Bach did. For saying something like that in these times makes one guilty of the kind of cheap journalism denounced by Karl Kraus. In such times someone like Wittgenstein has the experience of the solipsist in the *Tractatus:* He is right, but he cannot say so.

The illnesses that Wittgenstein diagnoses seem to others like strapping good health; much of what he recognizes as villainy others consider highly moral. What can be gleaned from the not-very-numerous comments by Wittgenstein on these things is an additional character trait, one often, inexplicably, overlooked: his boyish playfulness, the understated craftiness of his flashes of wit. In a completely unexpected passage from the *Remarks on the Foundations of Mathematics*, he says, with a perfectly straight face:

> The sickness of an age is healed through a change in the way of life of the people, and the sickness of the philosophical problems could only be healed through a changed way of thinking and living, not through a remedy discovered by an individual.

Imagine that the use of the car causes and further contributes to certain diseases, and that mankind is plagued by this disease until, for one reason or another, resulting from some development, people give up driving. (Part I, § 23).

The times are so sick that only a thoroughgoing change in the form of life itself can be of any help. (Those who consider Wittgenstein to be a thoroughgoing conservative should take special note here!) But because he expected no positive change, it was with "grave doubts" that he "passed on the *Philosophical Investigations* to the public":

That it should be given to this work in its meagerness and in the darkness of these times to shine a little light into one brain or another is not impossible; but it is certainly not likely.[27]

Wittgenstein rarely had a good opinion either of people in general or of the particular people among whom he found himself at any given time. Consider, for example, the following from a letter to Russell, written when he was teaching school:

I am still in Trattenbach and am still, as always, surrounded by ugliness and commonness. It is true that people on the average are not worth much anywhere, but here they are much more useless and irresponsible than anywhere else. (Oct. 23, 1921).

On another occasion, when Russell was on his way to give a speech at a congress dedicated to humanitarian goals and Wittgenstein showed his disapproval, Russell asked if he would prefer an organization for war and slavery. Whereupon Wittgenstein answered, "By far, by far!"

But even more than he mistrusted people, Wittgenstein mistrusted the idea that technical advances could help us

---

27. Although Wittgenstein always had problems with spelling and (above all) punctuation, occasionally his punctuation is masterful—for example, his use of the semicolon in this quotation, and in the above-quoted remark on the way the philosopher "treats" a question (*PI*, § 255).

in solving our real problems. This is nowhere expressed more concisely or humorously than in the following remark from one of the last notebooks: "People have reasoned that a king could make rain; *we* say this runs contrary to all experience. Today, people reason that the airplane, radio, etc., are a means of bringing the nations together and spreading culture" (*OC*, § 132).[28]

Wittgenstein felt at home in the cultural world of the first half of the nineteenth century; however, his relationship with the people and advances of his own time were problematical. He even had his difficulties with God. As a young man and as a student he was decidedly against religion and those who were its official representatives. Later (perhaps because of some "experience"), he came to understand the possibility of a religious life. During the war, he learned to pray and continued the practice later from time to time. Christian thought preoccupied him; the *Confessions* of Augustine and the *Vulgate* were for a long time among his favorite books. He was by no means a believing Christian, however, as the following remarks indicate:

> I read, "And no one can call Jesus 'Lord' except that he be led by the Holy Spirit."—And it is true: I can call no one *Lord* because that does not say anything to me. I could call him 'the example,' even 'God'—or more exactly, I can understand why people do that; but I cannot use the word 'Lord' meaningfully. *Because I do not believe* that he is coming to judge me, because *that* does not mean anything to me. And that could only mean something to me if I were to live my life *quite* differently. (1937, *CV*, p. 33).

One's religious conviction and one's life have to be in harmony, otherwise one's life would not be "decent." Wittgenstein's position on philosophy was no different. Only someone who could hope to make a contribution to philoso-

---

28. Wittgenstein attended a discussion in which somebody said: "With all the ugly sides of our civilization, I am sure I would rather live as we do now than have to live as the cave man did." To this he responded: "Yes of course you would. But would the cave man?" (Rhees, "Postscript," pp. 222–23).

phy should take up philosophy as a profession. Again and again, and with varying success, he attempted to persuade students to give up philosophy because he considered the academic climate to be dangerous. Only someone who was completely absorbed in the problems could be immune. All the same, he had a very businesslike attitude toward his own activities, but it was a "decent" businesslike attitude. In a letter written to Moore in mid-June 1929 he says bluntly:

> Supposing I was run over by a bus today and then were to see my tutor and say, "I'm a cripple for lifetime; couldn't the College give me some money to support me?" Then it would be right to ask the question: "And how long do you propose this to go on, and when will you be self-supporting?" But this is *not* my case. I propose to do work, and I have a vague idea that the College in some cases encourages such work by means of research grants, fellowships, etc. That's to say, I turn out some sort of goods, and *if* the College has any use for these goods, I would like the college to enable me to produce them, as long as it *has* use for them, and as long as I *can* produce them.—If, on the other hand, the College has no use for them, that puts an end to the question.

Still, Wittgenstein was on occasion quite helpless when it came to real financial problems or other practical concerns, having to turn for help to his friends Keynes or Sraffa. (Apparently he had managed to preserve a certain sense of optimism, at least with regard to the economy.) Because he had given away his own inheritance but still occasionally wanted to render financial assistance to certain persons, he had to turn to others on such occasions. It seemed quite natural to him to ask his well-to-do friends for such loans, grants, or gifts. Judging from the results, they must have found it just as natural to grant his requests.

Wittgenstein was indeed an imposing figure. Whoever reads the comments of his contemporaries, friends, students, and family members finds it downright tiring to hear again and again that he was "a true genius," "the most impressive man that I have ever met," "the most passionate thinker," "the most independent spirit," etc. But such comments have to be taken seriously because they were made by Russell, Keynes, Schlick, Leavis, and many others who were not that easily impressed.

In terms of his external appearance, however, Wittgenstein did not cut a dazzling figure. He had dressed with great care in the period before the war, but did not stand out for all that, judging from photographs. His facial expression was, as already mentioned, different after the war, and there was a change in the rest of his appearance as well. According to his sister Mining,

> ... he often created a strange impression because he took no notice of his personal appearance—for example he went around every day of the year and on all occasions in a brown coat, grey flannel pants (patched when possible), a shirt with open collar and no tie. But his serious face and energetic demeaner were so striking that everyone immediately saw the "gentleman" in him.[29]

That is a very direct but apparently quite accurate description. Everyone immediately saw the "gentleman" in him, and there seems to have been little interest on his part to change that.

He had, as numerous reports testify, thoroughly human habits. He was by no means an ascetic. He apparently made no big fuss about meals, preferring light foods because of constant stomach problems, but he always wanted his coffee strong and aromatic. Almost always doing whatever he wanted to, he would become angry should anyone threaten to interfere with one of his many prerogatives. He had a great many prejudices—against women and dogs, for example—but that is not unusual and only noted when the person in question is famous enough. He worked too much: Leavis gives us an impressive description of Wittgenstein in an overworked condition.[30] It is no wonder that he gradually adopted a routine that allowed

---

29. Hermine Wittgenstein, "My Brother Ludwig," pp. 9–10.

30. Leavis, "Memories of Wittgenstein," pp. 74–75.

him to keep philosophical problems at a distance for short periods of time. For example, he regularly read detective stories and went to the movies to relax after class or strenuous discussions. The following account by Drury is typical:

> After reading [Frazer's *The Golden Bough*], we often went to a cinema together, a "flick," as he always called it. He insisted on sitting in the very front row and would appear to be completely absorbed in the picture. He would go only to American films, and he expressed a dislike for all English and Continental ones: in these, the camera man was always intruding himself as if to say "Look how clever I am!" I remember him expressing a special delight in the dancing of Ginger Rogers and Fred Astaire.[31]

But even these harmless pleasures were means to the end of preserving an extremely sensitive spiritual balance. As he wrote in a moving letter to von Wright (February 21, 1947), he was unable to attend the latter's lectures "for the sole reason that in order to be able *to live* and *to work* I must not allow any foreign goods (i.e., philosophical goods) to enter my consciousness." And yet he was not at all convinced that the philosophical problems occupying his time were the most important. In one of his most remarkable notes he wrote the following:

> There are problems that I never approach, that are not in my line or in my world. Problems of Western thought that Beethoven (and perhaps Goethe too) approached and struggled with, but which no philosopher has ever addressed (perhaps Nietzsche noticed them). And perhaps they are lost to Occidental philosophy. . . .
>
> But I never come in contact with these problems. When I "have done with the world," I have created an amorphous (transparent) mass, and the world with all its diversity remains like an uninteresting lumber room somewhere off to the left.

---

31. Drury, "Conversations with Wittgenstein," p. 135.

Or, perhaps more accurately: the total result of all the work is leaving the world off to the left. (The throwing-into-the-junk-room of the whole world.) (1931, *CV*, p. 9).

Works

The table of contents in the German edition of Wittgenstein's collected works contains about twenty titles. There is, in addition, a list of shorter writings such as lecture notes and volumes of letters. The published writings do not include Wittgenstein's complete works by any means. The papers found after his death, which are still increasing in number, are said to total about 30,000 pages. The pages of these posthumous papers are, by and large, of varying format, and many are simply duplicates. But even if the number of pages shrinks to about 20,000 on closer examination, that would still mean that the bulk of Wittgenstein's writings is as yet unpublished.

This assertion is, to be sure, not entirely true since the greatest part of Wittgenstein's writings has been made public in a different form. A microfilm copy (and whatever paper copies have been made from it) does exist, which includes the greatest part of Wittgenstein's posthumous papers and is available in several university libraries. There is no better way to gain an insight into Wittgenstein's approach to his own work and, to a certain extent, into the way he thought, than to read some of his papers in the original. In so doing, one can see how Wittgenstein gradually changed his text, made alterations, crossed them out again, and reformulated them—how he constantly worked the same comments into different contexts in order to test an overall meaning, as it were. Reading the copies of the originals is, in most cases, not difficult to do. One does not need to be a practiced philologist nor terribly knowledgeable about Wittgenstein. The list of Wittgenstein's posthumous papers compiled by G. H. von Wright is useful in providing information on textual connections.[32] With its

---

32. von Wright, "The Wittgenstein Papers," pp. 35–62.

help one easily can find some manuscripts or typescripts on the microfilm (or the corresponding paper copy) and make textual comparisons of the pertinent parts. With the exception of occasional handwritten entries, the numerous typescripts offer no difficulties with legibility—and even the handwritten material is usually not difficult to read. Only a few manuscripts pose serious problems—but not everyone wants to read the entire twenty or thirty thousand pages anyway.

Two works by von Wright give exhaustive information on the origins of the *Tractatus* and the *Philosophical Investigations.*[33] But for the early stages and (more important) the editorial structuring of the other writings, there are not enough clues in either the notes of the various editors or in the secondary literature to make it clear to the reader why certain material belongs together. Much important work still must be done in this area, for a reliable edition of an author's writings is a prerequisite for dealing adequately with him.

It cannot be our purpose here to survey the history of all of the published writings of Wittgenstein. However, a few fundamental problems about the presentation of the texts affect the viewpoint of the readers and their understanding of the writings. We shall briefly address some of these fundamental problems, with a view to answering the question as to what is to count as a "work by Wittgenstein."

This question is somewhat ambiguous. It could mean "Is it a *work?*" or "Is it a work *by Wittgenstein?*" Certainly, the question whether something is a work by the author Wittgenstein may appear at first to be farfetched, even out of place. But in fact it is not unjustified, as a few examples may explain.

Except for the *Tractatus,* a short review, and the "Remarks on Logical Form," nothing published under Wittgenstein's name is free of editorial intervention.[34] The

---

33. "The Origin of the *Tractatus,*" pp. 63–109; and "The Origin and Composition of the *Philosophical Investigations,*" pp. 111–36.

34. Here the *Blue Book* and the *Brown Book* occupy an intermediate position, for these dictated texts were reproduced under Wittgenstein's

most glaring example is *Zettel,* a book presenting Peter
Geach's arrangement of remarks that Wittgenstein had cut
out of various typed manuscripts and saved in a box. A
further example is the *Philosophical Grammar,* in which
the editor (Rush Rhees) attempted to reconstruct a late
stage of the reworking of a typed manuscript from 1933,
but which ended up omitting extensive sections of the text—
sections that have remained unpublished. A third example
is the decision of the editors to edit Wittgenstein's last
manuscript in the form of two separate books, *Remarks on
Color* and *On Certainty*—although the manuscripts themselves suggest no such major division, and although a large
portion of the *Remarks on Color* obviously belongs, considering its content, to the themes of *On Certainty.*[35] In all the
cases just cited, as well as all the other posthumous publications, the question is to what extent the printed text is
directly attributable to Wittgenstein, and to what extent
the editors have changed the materials entrusted to them.
Generally speaking, Wittgenstein's words have been altered
in only a very few instances; however, the selection and
arrangement of his writings are more or less the work of
editors. So these publications are not fully the work of the
author Wittgenstein since they owe their shape and character to the editors.

Questions of this sort regarding the works of
Wittgenstein will not, however, be treated further in this
book. The aspects that concern us can perhaps be clearly
illustrated by a comparison with the works of other authors and especially by comparisons with artistic works.
Several of the symphonies of Bruckner, Wagner's
Tannhäuser, or Gottfried Keller's *Green Henry,* for example,
are works that exist in part in versions that are basically

---

own guidance for his students and a few friends (e.g., Russell). On the other
hand, Wittgenstein emphasized in a letter to Moore (probably December
1933), that there is "no reason in the world why we should have to make
more [than fifteen] copies."

35. The division into two "works" had the consequence that a part of this
highly interesting textual material is not yet published. (It is to be hoped
that it will soon come to light.)

different. In these cases one can certainly say which is the earlier and which is the later version, perhaps even which is the more exuberant and which is the more mature version, but that does not necessarily indicate which, or even if, one version is preferable to the other. It is not possible, however, to say of any of these examples that the different versions are different works, because the thematic material and extensive parts of the structural design are too similar. The situation is somewhat comparable to the various editions of some philosophical works, such as Locke's *Essay* or Kant's *Critique of Pure Reason*. Here one can hardly ignore the fact that the later versions contain corrections, more precise formulations, and elaborations that the author intended and which, to that extent, make them preferable to the earlier versions. Still it is not unreasonable to give a certain priority to the first edition of the *Critique of Pure Reason* (as, for example, Schopenhauer did).

The case of Wittgenstein's writings is different in that, with the exception of the *Tractatus,* the author did not publish them during his lifetime. But there are special cases—the *Philosophical Remarks,* for example. The typed manuscript on which the printed version is based was taken from several volumes of manuscripts in which Wittgenstein had selected and revised remarks, included them in a typed text, and worked them into a final reorganized text. In view of this preparatory work, and the fact that Wittgenstein wrote several forwards for the typed text, we may refer to the *Philosophical Remarks* as a tentatively completed "work."

Neither the manuscript, however, nor the typed text that was used in the preparatory work, are independent works or versions of one work. Let me give three reasons for this assertion: (1) It is easily recognizable that these writings are, from Wittgenstein's own point of view, preliminary stages of a more unified creation with a clearer structure. (2) These preliminary stages lack a more comprehensive line of argument that transcends the individual remarks. (3) These preliminary stages do not reveal the detail or overall stylistic refinement apparent in the *Philo-*

sophical Remarks. One could no more regard the preliminary stages of the *Philosophical Remarks* as earlier versions of the work than one could regard Beethoven's notes on the "Pastorale" as earlier versions of the symphony.

From another point of view, the *Philosophical Remarks* are just one of several versions of the work that Wittgenstein had wanted to write since his return to Cambridge in 1929. For practically everything Wittgenstein wrote beginning in this period was directed to writing a philosophical book—*the* book that would not only correct the *Tractatus* but also go beyond it in the treatment of new subjects. He states in the forward to the *Philosophical Investigations,* dated January 1945, that he was publishing "the precipitate of philosophical investigations" that had occupied him since 1929. These investigations, Wittgenstein continues, were concerned with the following subjects: "The concepts of meaning, of understanding, of the proposition, of logic, the foundations of mathematics, states of consciousness, and other things." This list of topics for the book is extremely revealing, especially if one considers that the topics of logic in the narrower sense, as well as the foundations of mathematics, are only intimated by way of examples or treated indirectly—as in the discussion of rules. These topics are discussed in the *Remarks on the Foundations of Mathematics,* written during the period extending from the end of the thirties through the first half of the forties. And we can safely assume that Wittgenstein would have included these discussions in the last version of the *Philosophical Investigations* if he had been sufficiently satisfied with them. That he had this intention is clear from the content and structure of the drafts of 1930 and 1933 (about which the printed versions of the *Philosophical Remarks* and the *Philosophical Grammar* provide information). In both cases all of the topics named in the preface to the *Philosophical Investigations* (see previous quote) are treated extensively, at times with entirely different emphases and, in part, completely different conclusions in the individual cases.

For a period of many years, it was most certainly the plan that the *Philosophical Investigations* too—as well as the *Philosophical Remarks* and the large typed manuscript of 1933[36]—was supposed to contain extensive remarks on the philosophy of mathematics and logic that would have, no doubt, been based essentially on the textual material in *Remarks on the Foundations of Mathematics*. Looking at it from this perspective, one could say that at least the *Philosophical Remarks*, the typed manuscript of 1933, and the first part of the *Philosophical Investigations* (possibly together with the *Remarks on the Foundations of Mathematics*), represent various versions of Wittgenstein's planned later work. Wittgenstein's statements in the preface to the *Philosophical Investigations*—for example, "It was my intention from the beginning to put all of this together in a book for which I envisioned different forms at different times"—also confirm the possibility of this.

These variations in Wittgenstein's conception of form become apparent when comparing "the big typescript" of 1933 with the first part of the *Philosophical Investigations*. While in the typescript the attempt is made to connect the material through chapter and section divisions and headings, in the *Investigations* Wittgenstein avoids any such organizational tools. Concerning the form, it was important to him that—as he says—"the thoughts proceed from one subject to another in a natural and seamless series." The remarks of the *Philosophical Investigations* thus constitute "a multitude of landscape sketches," as Wittgenstein puts it, a "picture" of the conceptual landscape traveled through, an "album."

The tone of Wittgenstein's statements in the preface to the *Philosophical Investigations* lets one see that he was not completely satisfied with the result, that he really had wanted something other than a "multitude of landscape sketches" or an "album." However, he was of the opinion that he would "never attain" this other something. That, of course, does not mean that the *Philosophical Investigations*—that is, its first part (he apparently did not want to

---

36. For the form, meaning, and problematic aspects of this typescript, see Kenny, "From the Big Typescript to the *Philosophical Grammar*," and Hilmy, *The Later Wittgenstein*, pp. 25–39.

print the second part in this manner together with the first)—are without form or inner coherence. It simply means that the design never quite comes up to Wittgenstein's ideal conception. The requirement of the "natural" and "seamless" series of thoughts is satisfied sufficiently for one to call the first part of the *Investigations,* in terms of formal arrangement, a "work" of Wittgenstein's.

These considerations make it possible to formulate positive criteria for calling something "a finished work of Wittgenstein's": (1) the assessment by Wittgenstein himself that the text in question is an independent creation with a form suitable to its content; (2) a line of argument apparent to the reader, with theses, arguments, objections, underlying considerations, and examples, etc.; and (3) the formal stylistic polishing and formulation of the text which make it possible to call it "finished" or "complete."

If we apply these standards to Wittgenstein's writings, the following picture emerges: First, a number of notebooks clearly have the character of sketches or tentative experiments. Second, numerous "volumes," as Wittgenstein himself called them, often are based on material from the notebooks but are stylistically better formulated in argument and formal structure, only rarely revealing a larger line of argument.[37] Third, there are texts in which the material of the first two phases has been somewhat "filtered" but which still do not reveal any more comprehensive argumentative and formal line. And finally, some writings remain that fulfill the above-mentioned three criteria; these, and only these, are properly called "works."

This clearly graduated picture is clouded somewhat by the fact that Wittgenstein was never quite satisfied with what he wrote.[38] Immediately upon presenting even

---

37. Of course the "volumes" (or parts of "volumes") containing fair copies or revisions are not to be included in these.

38. This fact about Wittgenstein is attested to forcefully by his collaborator of many years, Friedrich Waismann. Waismann wrote: "He [Wittgenstein] has the marvelous gift of always seeing everything as if for the first time. But I think it's obvious how difficult any collaboration is, since he always follows the inspiration of the moment and demolishes what he has previously planned" (*WVC*, Preface, p. 26).

the "most finished" typed manuscript, he habitually started to rewrite, or else abandoned it in disappointment, changing the topic of his investigations. It might therefore be appropriate to regard the writings of the fourth category—which I want to designate as "works" despite this reservation—not really as the conclusion of a development during a certain time, but rather as deposits of sediment in a current that slackens and rises at certain points but then seeks another kind of riverbed and flows on. As soon as Wittgenstein begins rewriting a work, things are again in flux, and as long as they are in flux, we are no longer dealing with a "work" in the sense intended here but with the building blocks of a work in progress.

These considerations show that the "work" concept cannot be applied without reservation to the published and unpublished writings of Wittgenstein. For example, the *Philosophical Remarks* are obsolete to the extent that they present an earlier version of the texts that appear in later years. And we must certainly not forget that, at least for a brief period of time, Wittgenstein regarded the *Philosophical Remarks,* the "big typescript" of 1933, or the prewar version of the *Philosophical Investigations* as a preliminary conclusion. And he accepted even the last version of the *Investigations* only because he saw no possibility of making it better. Therefore, if we wish to designate the *Philosophical Remarks* and the *Philosophical Investigations,* for example, as works of Wittgenstein, we must not create the impression that we are dealing with a continuous progression in Wittgenstein's philosophical development—constant progress from one work to the next with their clearly appropriate sketches, drafts, and preliminary stages. For the deposits of sediment in the flow of the philosophical investigations of Wittgenstein, which with some justification can be called works, are at the same time also interruptions in the current; they are the points where Wittgenstein—probably because of his awareness of unsolved problems and unresolved difficulties—decided on an entirely new approach; they are the points at which the river seeks out a new riverbed.

The questions about what is to be regarded as a "work" of Wittgenstein's and how his writings should be read also can be approached by considering what a critical edition of his collected writings would have to be. In order to be able to edit posthumous papers into a useful form, there have to be certain boundary markers, for the writings have to be arranged as preliminary or subsequent, sketches or reflections; otherwise there can be no external—and to that extent, objective—criteria for presenting the text.

Usually such boundary markers for the development of works are visibly and clearly set by the authors themselves through publication or manuscript completion. It is just these aids to orientation that are missing in Wittgenstein's case since he neither published his texts (with the exception of the *Tractatus*) nor expressed his clear satisfaction with his manuscripts.

There are some inescapable conclusions. On the one hand, editions of these writings must not even give the appearance of being "works" since the author himself could not, or did not wish to, consider them completed works. On the other hand, an edition of so many manuscripts and typescripts without certain accents and breaks would be inaccessible to any reader. (Books should be read after all—something editors often forget!) And one cannot simply follow a chronological order and automatically take the more recent to be the more perfected or more complete, for such a judgement in the case of Wittgenstein would be clearly mistaken.[39]

The only possibility seems to me to be the following: Use criteria, such as those briefly described above, and look at the writings not so much as something finished and complete but rather as "experiments." Then one can (to give an example) call the typed manuscript of "Remarks II,"[40] written around the time of the typescript of *Philo-*

---

39. Here it is to be borne in mind that, now and then, Wittgenstein disregarded the reworked text and went back to an earlier version.

40. Cf. von Wright, "The Origin and Composition of the *Philosophical Investigations*," pp. 132–33. "*Bemerkungen II*" contains for the most part the same textual materials as the final two thirds of Part I of the

sophical Investigations, Part I, a somewhat less successful experiment than the latter. It cannot be denied, however, that Wittgenstein's thoughts were deposited as sediment in his unpublished writing as well; and it is our good fortune that eventually everything began to flow again as the current sought out another riverbed. But that does not alter the fact that for a time it did move in the direction indicated in the unpublished typescript, and that the current did flow in that manner is something about which we should know.

Investigations, yet the particular remarks are quite differently arranged. Von Wright comes to the following conclusion: *"Bemerkungen II* is definitely an arrangement with a view to subject matter. With some justification *Bemerkungen II* may be regarded as an independent and final work by Wittgenstein" (p. 132).

2

***

Tractatus Logico-Philosophicus

How to Read the *Tractatus*

In approaching this difficult book a few pointers should be kept in mind, the first concerning its often-imitated numbering system. Wittgenstein explains that the decimal numbers assigned to the individual propositions indicate their "logical weight," "the emphasis placed on them in my exposition." This means that, by giving prominence to certain propositions—those numbered 1, 2, 3, etc., and next 1.1, 1.2, 2.1, 2.2, etc.—the numbering system provides path markers for reading. It does not mean that the primary numbers (1, 2, etc.) are related to the subordinate (1.1, etc.) as premises to conclusion. The propositions of the *Tractatus* are, in fact, seldom related in this way, for understanding them requires reading "from above to below" as well as "from below to above." Another point: it would be wrong to think that the number of decimal places always gives the "absolute logical weight" of a proposition; thus the proposition expressing the "fundamental thought" of the book has the number 4.0312. (It almost appears that Wittgenstein wanted to hide this "fundamental thought" of his.) In sum: the *Tractatus* numbering is useful in gaining an overview of themes; otherwise it is to be regarded with suspicion.

The *Tractatus* is now about seventy years old. Thus, in order to understand it better, we have to take into account many of those factors that were obvious or may have been

taken for granted at the time of its writing and publication. One cannot profitably read the book without a certain
knowledge of the logical fundamentals, knowledge that is
much more widespread now than at the time of the publication of the *Tractatus.* And those who lack such information can readily obtain it from one of countless good text-
books.

The *Tractatus* hardly presupposes a knowledge of the
history of philosophy, but Wittgenstein's acknowledgment
in the preface must be considered: "I will only mention
that many of my thoughts were stimulated by the great
works of Frege and by the writings of my friend Mr.
Bertrand Russell." In fact, a lot in the *Tractatus* is not
completely intelligible until one has taken into account
certain ideas and formulations of Frege and, even more so,
Russell's specific way of presenting a problem. An example
of this is Russell's theory of judgement mentioned in 5.5422,
presented in a manuscript[41] that did not appear in complete form until 1984. (Russell had suppressed the manuscript because of Wittgenstein's criticism.)

Occasionally one hears that other authors in addition
to Frege and Russell are important for an adequate understanding of the *Tractatus,* for example Schopenhauer and
the physicist Heinrich Hertz. It is correct that Hertz's *Principles of Mechanics* (as well as the writings of Boltzmann)
stood godfather for a few of the ideas of the *Tractatus* (cf.
4.04, 6.361; *NB,* 12/6/14). It is also true that Wittgenstein
took over many formulations from Schopenhauer; perhaps
he had Schopenhauer's works at hand while working on
the manuscript of 1916/17 (*NB,* pp. 71ff.). These authors
did in fact have an influence on Wittgenstein, and their
influence is important; however, knowledge of their works
is not a necessary prerequisite for understanding
Wittgenstein's text.

Of greatest importance for an understanding the
Tractatus is the matter of style. Probably around the middle

---

41. Russell, *The Theory of Knowledge.* Cf. Pears, "The Relation Between
Wittgenstein's Picture Theory of Propositions and Russell's Theories of
Judgment."

of October 1919, Wittgenstein wrote to Ludwig von Ficker: "The work is strictly philosophical and literary at the same time; however, there is no gassing in it." The literary element would strike even the casual reader. What stands out is the extreme compression of the wording. And yet it would not be quite right to call his style aphoristic, for even though Wittgenstein's reading of Nietzsche and Lichtenberg was certainly not without effect, his sentences are without the intentional sparkle typical of aphorists, and his train of thought is without their occasional playfulness. Wittgenstein wants to hit the nail on the head with every formulation, as he tells us in the preface. At the same time he tries to convey something through the tone of the whole work, something that cannot, he thinks, be abruptly expressed. That there is no "gassing" in the *Tractatus* is a stylistic virtue. The laconic seriousness of the tone indirectly conveys the message that "gassing" *must* be avoided. Thus Wittgenstein intends not only to clear up certain misunderstandings in the logic of language, but also (and at the same time) to condemn the misuse of language—an intention he shares with Karl Kraus.

Philosophy

In a conversation with Waismann at the end of 1931,[42] Wittgenstein said that a dangerous mistake permeated the *Tractatus*, namely, the idea that one could treat some philosophical questions as if the answer would be found at some time in the future. The mistake was comparing philosophical problems to problems of the natural sciences, thereby reading something hypothetical into them and into their possible solutions. He went on to explain that he had not made this error because his earlier philosophical concepts had been false or insufficient. He said that already during the work on his book he had written—but not included in the final text—remarks such as: "The solutions of the philo-

---

42. See the extensive quotation at the beginning of chapter 3.

sophical problems must never come as a surprise. Nothing
can be discovered in philosophy" (*WVC*, pp. 182f.). He said
that his mistake was in not sufficiently taking to heart his
own insights into the task of philosophy.

Indeed, the 1913 "Notes on Logic" already contain statements on the nature and task of philosophy that not only
anticipate many a formulation of the *Tractatus* but also
presage, in some respects, the ideas of the later period.
That philosophy is basically different from the natural sciences is already stated in the early text:

> Philosophy can neither confirm nor confute scientific
> research. . . . Philosophy is the doctrine of the logical form
> of scientific propositions (not just of primitive propositions).
> The word philosophy should always designate something
> that stands over or under, but not next to, the natural
> sciences. (*NB*, p. 106).

Similar statements are found in 4.111ff. of the *Tractatus*,
where the difference between philosophy and the natural
sciences is stressed and the actual task of philosophy more
exactly outlined:

> The purpose of philosophy is the logical clarification of
> thoughts.
>
> Philosophy is not a teaching but an activity.
>
> A philosophical work consists mainly of elucidations.
>
> The result of philosophy is not 'philosophical propositions',
> but the clarification of propositions.
>
> Philosophy should take thoughts that are otherwise turbid
> and blurred, so to speak, and make them clear and sharp.
> (4.112).

Revealing differences exist between the conception of
the *Tractatus* and the ideas of the 1913 "Notes." Thus we
read in the latter that philosophy contains no deductions
and is purely descriptive—which is a startling anticipation
of the much later statement, "We must get rid of all expla-

nation, putting only description in its place" (*PI*, § 109). But in the *Tractatus* "description," in the sense intended here, is not present (although the "elucidations" mentioned in 4.112 may in some respects resemble it). An additional difference is apparent when one examines the following note from 1913: "Philosophy consists of logic and metaphysics; logic is its basis." This cannot be reconciled with the *Tractatus*, which certainly also emphasizes the determining role of logic but is antimetaphysical in its intention and says so:

> The correct method of philosophy would be to say nothing except what can be said, namely, propositions from natural science—and therefore something having nothing to do with philosophy—and then whenever someone wanted to say something metaphysical, to show him that he had given no meaning to certain signs in his sentences. This method would not be satisfying to the other person—he would not have the feeling that we were teaching him philosophy—but it would be the only strictly correct method. (6.53).

Again the contrast between natural science and philosophy is underlined; at the same time he declares that philosophy must tolerate *nothing* metaphysical.

And yet the remark at 6.53 makes it strikingly clear that Wittgenstein, for his part, had no intention of abiding by the method of philosophy that he himself held to be the right one. For the *Tractatus* certainly does not consist of propositions from natural science; rather, it says what, according to 6.53, cannot be said. But, although he uses "nonsensical" sentences, "pseudo-propositions," this is far from saying that Wittgenstein is doing metaphysics. The *Tractatus* proceeds indirectly: remarks that are meaningless from its point of view are supposed to put the reader in a position to attain a sort of understanding for himself that cannot be presented in a systematic theory. Metaphysics is, in this view, a formal, systematic theory imitating natural science but (unlike natural science) necessarily mired in senselessness because of its language and theme.

However, it would be a short-sighted misunderstanding to ascribe to Wittgenstein the desire to abolish philosophy. One who has recognized the sentences of the *Tractatus* as nonsense, and thrown them away as the ladder on which he has ascended (6.54), does not thereupon have to limit himself to expressing propositions from natural science. To be consistent, he must apply the knowledge acquired to his own thinking and to his involvement with the thoughts of others. The answers to scientific questions leave life's problems untouched; moreover, meaningful questions cannot even be asked ("and this is exactly the answer," 6.52). Yet philosophy, as the activity that helps to clarify one's own propositions as well as the expressions of other speakers, is manifestly legitimate. What this conception requires cannot be explicated without speaking nonsense again; however, he who overlooks it when reading the *Tractatus* will necessarily miss the intention of the book.

It is, therefore, a misunderstanding to interpret the *Tractatus* as either a presentation of a systematic ontology or a treatise exclusively on the logical syntax of language. There are, to be sure, hints of ontological motifs, and insights into syntax do play a significant role; however, these hints and insights have an ancillary function only. Wittgenstein writes as early as the first paragraph of the preface that the *Tractatus* is not a textbook—a warning needed to offset the impression given by the rigid numbering system and the dogmatic tone, which Wittgenstein himself was later to deplore.

Philosophy does not become a science through the process of clarifying the logic of language; rather, it contributes to the delineation of the boundaries between science and everything else that one thinks one is capable of saying or thinking:

> Philosophy defines the controversial domain of natural science.
>
> It should fix the limits of the thinkable and, thereby, also of the unthinkable.
>
> It should define the unthinkable from within, by way of the thinkable. (4.113f.).

According to the preface, no boundaries can be described for thinking itself, because to do that one would have to be able to think the unthinkable. Philosophical activity is to limit itself to the *expression* of thoughts, that is, to that which can be said and, in fact, is said: "It will only be in language that the boundary can be set, and whatever lies beyond the boundary will simply be nonsense." Accordingly, the business of philosophy is critique. Like Kant, whom Wittgenstein revered, and who wanted to show the limits of human knowledge, Wittgenstein attempts to make the limits of meaningful speech clear through his investigations of the logic of language. But, in contrast to Kant, who wanted to place knowledge on a secure foundation, Wittgenstein's investigations end in mysticism and silence. Wittgenstein's indirect procedure is singular; the direction of thrust in his method is so difficult to make out that it appears, at times, to be its exact opposite—that of dogmatic metaphysics.

The first sentence of the preface should provide the occasion for much thought: "Perhaps only he who himself has had such thoughts as are expressed in this book will understand it." A deceptively simple statement that is too easily ignored. Yet, like every preface of Wittgenstein's, this one contains no superfluous language; it places the text that follows it in a very personal light. It is therefore advisable to consider carefully the tone established in the preface. If the claim often attributed to the book were true, namely that it purports to provide an ontological, metaphysical system or, more modestly, a treatise suitable for schools on the logical syntax of language (or a language), then the first sentence of the preface would be incomprehensible. For why should the reader of such a work need already to have had the thoughts expressed in it? The reader of a book on logic or of a metaphysical system expects something new and hopes to be instructed; it does not occur to him that having thoughts similar to the author's might be a prerequisite for understanding his statements. But Wittgenstein does indeed want to say that readers can understand the book only if they have, at some time, thought approximately the same way as he did. Of course, Wittgenstein cannot mean his own specific terminology ("object," "states of affairs and facts," "name," "elementary proposition," "proposition," etc.), for hardly a reader will have thought of such things in advance. And it is equally difficult to see why one needs to have had a particular thought experience in order to be able to understand this terminology. So Wittgenstein must mean thoughts of a different kind. As to *what* kind of thoughts he did have in mind, a possible answer will be suggested later, in the last section of this chapter.

The third sentence of the preface is not much less confusing than the first, for it says that the purpose of the book "would be achieved if it gave pleasure to one who read it with understanding." Anyone who knows how grimly serious most of the interpretations of the *Tractatus* are has to smile sadly on reading this sentence. But aside from that, who would ever have thought that the "purpose" of a philosophical book could consist of giving "pleasure" to the reader? In the face of the objective difficulty of the text, of which even Wittgenstein was well aware,[43] a kind of irony could be imputed to the author. But that is surely not the whole story. Wittgenstein wants to lead the reader to a certain point through the book's style, as well as through hinting at its intention; he wants to influence the reader's personal attitude, winning him over and obtaining his consent regarding certain matters not open to meaningful discussion. Therefore, he is seeking to stimulate a reaction akin to an aesthetic pleasure that cannot be completely articulated in words. If this reaction is elicited, then, according to the author, the purpose of the book has been achieved.

World

The *Tractatus* begins with some weighty pronouncements: "The world is everything that is the case. The world

---

43. For example, Wittgenstein wrote to Russell on August 19, 1919, that Frege had understood "not a word" of the whole book, adding that it would

is the totality of facts, not of things. The world is determined by the facts, and by their being *all* the facts." But what world is being spoken of here? Whoever looks around and sees desk, pencil, chairs, flowers, trees, people, cars may retort that what he sees is certainly part of the real world—the part manifestly consisting of the things just mentioned. How can Wittgenstein insist that the world is *not* the totality of things but of facts? *That* the pencil is lying on the table, *that* the flowers are standing on the windowsill, these are facts. But does one really perceive facts—in the same sense that one perceives at one time the table, at another time the flowers, and then again something else? This objection assumes an "atomic theory" of perception, according to which the world consists of large and small, clearly defined, fragments. But is that assumption correct?

As soon as one reflects on it, one sees that the assumption is not as natural as it may have seemed. For I do not perceive the table and the other things as isolated; rather, what I perceive always has a certain order. I see that the table is to the left of the window, that the pencil is on the table, that the flowers are behind the curtain. That is not, of course, to say that I see "the being to the left," "the being on X or behind Y." We want to say, rather, that the world of which Wittgenstein speaks is somehow orderly.

Parallel to the world of perception just characterized, the world of the *Tractatus* does not consist of isolated fragments and lumps. It is arranged according to "that" clauses; in other words, it "breaks down into facts" (1.2).

The statement that the world of the *Tractatus* is structured according to such "that" clauses and breaks down into facts, however, does not by any means say everything about Wittgenstein's peculiar concept of the world. At 1.21 he says, "Something can be the case or not be the case while everything else remains the same." That sounds misleading, for if the pencil is not on the table but in my

---

be "*very* hard not to be understood by a single soul." He really should not have been surprised by the lack of comprehension: already on June 12 he had written to Russell that it would be galling to think "that no one will understand it even if it does get printed."

pocket, then not "everything else" can remain the same. I must have taken the pencil, for example, and placed it in my pocket. At least, that is the way things are in our normal world in which things move only when there is a cause; and as soon as causality enters in, everything seems linked to everything else. Changes do not take place without all sorts of things happening. If there is a new fact, a "complete" causal description of the world has to mention a lot of things; it is surely not as if everything else remained the same. The obvious conclusion is, therefore, that the world of the *Tractatus* is not a world of causal description and, consequently, not—or not essentially—a world in space and time. And just that could follow from 1.13: "The facts in logical space are the world." For logical space is surely not identical with the empirical space of sensory experience or of a physical theory.

So far we know: The world of the *Tractatus* is organized according to "that" clauses. It breaks down into facts, but these are not the facts of experience or of physics because they are not dependent on or linked to one another according to a causal description. And yet Wittgenstein insists that "the world" of which he speaks is nothing other than total reality (2.063). But is reality not the same as the empirical world of space, time, and causality?

Signs

Reality, it says in 2.06, is the existence or nonexistence of states of affairs. But what are states of affairs? Are they not the same as facts? According to 2.01, states of affairs are combinations of objects (matters, things). A fact is: that things behave in a certain manner—that certain states of affairs exist. Here a vague difference between state of affairs and fact is suggested. For an explanation we must clarify a few peculiarities in the terminology of the *Tractatus*. To Russell, who had asked for a clarification of the difference between state of affairs and fact, Wittgenstein wrote the following in a letter dated August 19, 1919: "Sachverhalt [state of affairs] is what corresponds to an Elementarsatz [elementary proposition] if it is true. Tatsache [fact] is what corresponds to the logical product of elementary propositions when this product is true." The explanation is moved to another level, so to speak—the level of language. We can better understand "state of affairs" and "fact" if we clarify "elementary proposition," "proposition," and a few other terms. A fact, according to Wittgenstein's explanation, corresponds to a conjunction (= logical product) of elementary propositions, as long as this conjunction (e.g., "p · q · r")—hence, each of its components ("p," "q," "r")—is true.

Elementary propositions are obviously not ordinary propositions. We may not replace the above variables "p," "q," "r," etc., with English propositions such as "The table is to the left of the window." Elementary propositions are, among other things, characterized by the fact that they cannot contradict one another (4.211). This means, in the first place, that they contain no logical particles [for example, "or," "not"], for if they did, they would be able to contradict one another. In the second place, it means that their components exhibit no complexity that can be so stated or reformulated that the deduction of a contradiction is possible. Accordingly, ordinary language terms such as "table," "to the left of," and such do not occur in elementary propositions. What remains? 4.22 provides the answer. "Elementary propositions consist of names. They are combinations, linkings of names."

That sounds as if an elementary proposition were something like the direct joining of expressions like "Peter," "Paul," "Louise," "Rome," "Berlin," and "Paris," so that an elementary proposition would sound something like "Peter-Rome-Louise," or "Paul-Paris-Louise-Berlin." These, assuming certain conventions, could be rendered "Peter is driving to Rome with Louise," or "Paul is driving from Paris to Louise in Berlin"; assuming other conventions, they could be rendered "Louise is taller than Peter," "Paul is meeting Louise from Berlin in Paris." But this interpretation cannot be quite right, for two reasons. In the first place, the "names" that occur in elementary propositions—and exclusively in elementary propositions (4.23)—are of a

STATE AFAIRS = ELEMENTARY PROPOSITION

completely different nature from everyday names; in the second place, conventions—to the extent that on this level they play any part at all in Wittgenstein's conception—cannot function in the way presented here. Unlike a code, elementary propositions obey no explicitly agreed-upon rules of application.

The names that occur in the elementary propositions are "primitive signs" (3.26) that cannot be more exactly defined. Names like "Paul" and "Rome," whose correct usage can be explained linguistically (through definition or definite description) are not names in the sense intended by Wittgenstein. Names that are themselves primitive signs designate in a completely different way from signs defined by means of primitive signs. We can assume that primitive signs do not occur at all in a proposition in the way they occur in the spoken or written words of our everyday language. Perhaps they can be indicated schematically, but otherwise their function is recognizable only through the application of the linguistic sign. The primitive signs themselves are "swallowed up" by the signs (cf. 3.262). Nevertheless, Wittgenstein states in 3.263 that "the meaning of the primitive signs is explained through elucidations. Elucidations are propositions containing the primitive signs. They can, therefore, be understood only when the meaning of these is already known."

Whenever "meaning" [*Bedeutung*] is spoken of in the *Tractatus,* it should be noted that this expression is used in a very specific sense: "The name means the object. The object is its meaning" (3.203). Wittgenstein uses the word "meaning" in a manner similar to Frege[44] in the sense of "that to which the expression refers." But Wittgenstein's application of the word "sense" [*Sinn*] is more like the everyday application. That has implications for the interpretation of 3.263, quoted in the previous paragraph (a

---

44. It is not without irony that Wittgenstein uses a formulation of Frege's in 3.3. (Compare the repeatedly-expressed "context principle" in Frege, *The Foundations of Arithmetic*—p. x, §§ 60, 62, 106, etc.). For he denies Frege's view that (like names) propositions have "sense" [*Sinn*] as well as "meaning" [*Bedeutung*]: "Only a proposition has sense; only in the context of a proposition does a name have meaning."

passage belonging to the most controversial material in the *Tractatus*), for one's understanding of "meaning" will vary according to the way one conceives "elucidation." A careful interpretation, one (as it seems to me) consistent with many other pronouncements of Wittgenstein, is given at 3.263: In order to understand what primitive signs mean, we must already be familiar with how they are used; in other words, in order to understand the reference of the primitive signs, we must be able to recognize on the basis of sample propositions what they refer to.

Here arises the problem of what sort of objects the primitive signs ("names") refer to. Although Wittgenstein said a lot about his objects—they are simple; they form the substance (the fixed form) of the world; they contain the possibility of all states of affairs—there is no unanimity among interpreters about their constitution. Roughly, three interpretations are distinguishable:

(1) Objects are to be viewed realistically—as though they were physical (or otherwise real) atoms, that is, entities entering into various compositions but intrinsically unchangeable.

(2) Objects are sense data, elements in the individual's perceptual field.

(3) Objects possess no independent existence; their nature is to be understood only by way of the function of the expressions designating them.[45]

It is significant that the *Tractatus* permits three basically different *kinds* of interpretation of "object." And although there is no space for an adequate discussion, we cannot help but note that the very existence of such differing interpretations seems to indicate the correctness of the third, the only one compatible with a certain indecisiveness regarding the nature of objects.

45. To fill out these briefly-sketched interpretations, see: (1) Malcolm, *Nothing is Hidden;* Pears, *The False Prison;* (2) Hintikka, *Investigating Wittgenstein;* (3) Ishiguro, "Use and Reference of Names"; McGuinness, "The So-Called Realism of Wittgenstein's *Tractatus*"; Winch, "Language, Thought and World in Wittgenstein's *Tractatus.*"

Analysis and Picture

Faced with this confusing plethora of interpretative possibilities and the quite bizarre terminology, one naturally asks the purpose of such complicated, theoretically-odd material. The answer lies partly in the critical nature of philosophical activity, mentioned earlier. It is a matter of distinguishing sense from nonsense, of discerning the boundary between what can be said and what cannot (really) be said. This task naturally assumes a very definite conception of language and the possibility of communicating thoughts. In 4.002 Wittgenstein describes his conception:

> We can create a language capable of expressing every sense without having any idea what each word means or how it has meaning—just as we can speak without knowing how the individual sounds are produced.
>
> Everyday language is part of the human organism and no less complicated.
>
> It is humanly impossible to infer the logic of language directly from language.
>
> Language cloaks thought, and does so to such an extent that from the exterior appearance of the cloak one cannot divine the concealed thought. For the cloak is not designed to reveal the form of the body but for entirely different ends.
>
> The tacit conventions needed for understanding everyday language are enormously complicated.

It is "humanly impossible" directly to infer the logic of language. Thus to explain it, thereby coming to understand its mode of functioning, calls for analysis. And analysis calls for the use of an instrument. Helping us at the same time to avoid language-related mistakes often committed by philosophers, this instrument is "a sign language governed by *logical* grammar, logical syntax" (3.325)—a symbolic language which, according to Wittgenstein, is an elaboration of the "concept-script" devised by Frege and developed by Russell. Wittgenstein's model here is undoubtedly Russell's "theory of descriptions." In quite a surpris-

ing manner, this theory provides a way of analyzing definite descriptions—"the author of *Faust*" or "the inventor of
the perpetual motion machine," for instance—so that their
real form is no longer "cloaked." (Russell's analysis shows
how sentences containing definite descriptions can always
be assigned a truth value ["true" or "false"]. This provides
a means of avoiding many philosophical problems regarding the function of "non-denoting expressions" [such as "inventor of the perpetual motion machine"]).

Wittgenstein wants to do more than improve the logical notation and analytical insights of Frege and Russell,
however. He wants to determine the elements that are at
the foundations of language—the irreducible components
at the last step of analysis. He assumes that such an analysis is possible but regards himself as unable to carry it out.
Putting the matter very briefly: Wittgenstein's elementary
propositions and primitive signs ("names") rest on a merely
assumed determinateness of linguistic sense. ("The demand
for the possibility of simple signs is the demand for the
determinateness of sense" [3.23].) As Wittgenstein himself
later admits, it is precisely at this point that he violates
his own basic principle that in philosophy there is nothing
to be discovered.

One must not think that Wittgenstein's linguistic-ana-
lytical approach is based on nothing more than an unjustified assumption. Its true strength lies in the totality of the
perceptions, analyses, conjectures, and metaphors presented
so concisely in the *Tractatus*. The persuasive power of the
Tractatus, the fascination felt by many contemporaries (for
example Russell, Ramsey, Schlick, and Carnap), stems from
the fact that all elements of the presentation—the quasi-
ontological propositions at the beginning, the picture theory,
the theory of truth functions, the reflections on the theory
of generality, and the mysticism—seem to point to the same
solution, even if this solution ultimately resists complete
revelation. "The chorus points to a secret law" (to use a
verse from Goethe that Wittgenstein quotes later).

If what we are thinking has meaning, we form propositions that can be expressed and can promote understanding. According to the *Tractatus*, propositions are pictures

of reality. Their pictorial character becomes especially clear in a schematic presentation. The sign "aRb" has the effect of a visible reproduction of the fact that object a stands in the relationship R to the object b. However, our normal propositions hardly reveal the pictorial character so clearly. In order to disclose the picture in the proposition, logical analysis must separate the representational elements in the proposition from the purely logical components. While the logical components make the presentation possible in the first place, they have no depicting function of their own. In this connection Wittgenstein employs instructive examples:

> 4.013. And when we delve into the essential nature of this pictorial character, we see that it is *not* impaired by *apparent irregularities* (such as the use of the # and b in musical notation).
>
> For even these irregularities depict that which they are intended to express; only they do it in a different way.
>
> 4.014. The gramophone record, the musical idea, the musical notation, the sound waves—all stand to each other in the same internal relation of depicting that holds between language and world.
>
> The logical structure is common to all.
>
> (Like the two youths in the fairy-tale, their two horses, and their lilies. All are in a certain sense one.)

This quotation shows that the picture character that Wittgenstein is concerned with is not modeled on photographs or sketches. The musical score cannot be interpreted as a photograph of the symphonic sounds. That there is a pictorial relationship between them is established by convention, rules, and practice. The musical notes are in no obvious sense similar to the sounds; in the same sense the youths bear just as little resemblance to their horses or the lilies.

No less important is the choice of examples—music, fairy tales; these makes it clear that the pictorial relationship meant by Wittgenstein is not a matter of simple similarity. Moreover, what he says about metaphors (4.015) and models (4.01) indicates that the intended pictorial character is not to be understood in the sense of an objective copy. The important thing is the agreement on the point of "logical (mathematical) multiplicity": "There must be as many distinguishable features in the proposition as there are in the situation it describes" (4.04). An expressionistic portrait will not pass for a photograph; however, it may possess the right logical multiplicity to reflect a certain attitude or mood, even though the colors it uses are not exactly those of the subject. The musical notation of some compositions by John Cage is not suitable for a symphony by Mozart, while it has exactly the right mixture of vagueness and ligature for the presentation of Cage's ideas. These examples illuminate the constructive and usage-dependent element of language stressed by Wittgenstein: "The proposition constructs a world" (4.023); "In the proposition a situation is, as it were, tentatively assembled" (4.031).

The diversity required for the pictorial function cannot, for its part, be the object of the pictorial representation: "Of course this mathematical multiplicity cannot itself be depicted. One cannot step outside of it when depicting" (4.041). This conviction has as much to do with Wittgenstein's rejection of Russell's theory of types, and the concept of graduated levels of language (object language, metalanguage), as it does with his own preference for a "palpable," "graphic" presentation of logic. The truth table (4.31), the schema (5.101), and the representation (6.1203) are supposed—each in its own way—to make the logical as *clear* as possible, without talking about it. The logical element—that which gives the picture its appropriate multiplicity—cannot itself become the object of a picture. The motto, "Logic has to take care of itself" (5.473; *NB*, p. 2 [8/22/14]) is based on the same idea—an idea also expressed in the remark containing the "fundamental idea" of the *Tractatus:*

> 4.0312. The possibility of the proposition rests on the principle of representing objects through signs. My fundamental idea is that the "logical constants" do not represent—that the *logic* of facts cannot be represented.

That which cannot be represented, and so cannot be represented by means of a picture, does not, as a consequence, necessarily remain concealed. *It shows itself*:

> 4.121. The proposition cannot represent logical form; logical form is reflected in it.
>
> That which is reflected in language cannot be represented by language.
>
> That which expresses *itself* in language cannot be expressed *by us* through language.
>
> The proposition *shows* the logical form of reality.
>
> It exhibits it.

Logical form, in which proposition and reality agree, and without which representations of reality are impossible, must therefore derive from the use of language. However, further linguistic formulation is inappropriate for the purpose of elucidating logical form. For what becomes apparent only through use cannot be described; it can at most be elucidated through a schematic model. Herein lies the significance of a clear logical notation, and of a reduction to the fewest possible elements. The reduction of all truth functions culminates in the single operation of the simultaneous negation of elementary propositions (5.5ff.). This reduction proceeds with an increasingly schematic characterization of the general form of the proposition:

> 4.5. . . . The general form of the proposition is: This is how things stand.
>
> 5. The proposition is a truth function of elementary propositions.
>
> (The elementary proposition is a truth function of itself.)
>
> 6. The general form of the truth function is:
>
> $$[\bar{p}, \bar{\xi}, N(\bar{\xi})].^{46}$$
>
> This is the general form of the proposition.

---

46. Here Wittgenstein falls back on notation used, above all, in remarks 5.25ff. and 5.5ff. Relying on Max Black, the bracketed formula can be

It is, consequently, a rule of operation meant to explain the general form of the proposition.

Saying and Showing—Logic

The preceding considerations help to bring a very distinct idea into focus. Wittgenstein puts it this way in a letter to Russell dated August 19, 1919:

> The main point is the theory of what can be expressed (gesagt) by prop[osition]s—i.e. by language—(and, which comes to the same, what can be *thought*) and what can not be expressed by prop[osition]s, but only shown (gezeigt); which, I believe, is the cardinal problem of philosophy.

Propositions that say something can be either true *or* false. That is to say, if one indicates their truth conditions through the letters T (= true) and F (= false), then in indicating these truth conditions both the T and the F must appear in the last column of the truth table. If one presents the proposition "It is raining or it is sunny" in the schematic form "p ∨ q" ("p" for "It is raining"; "q" for "It is sunny"; "∨" for "or"), the truth possibilities are:

p	q	∨
T	T	T
T	F	T
F	T	T
F	F	F

The last column under the disjunctive sign "∨" yields the series *TTTF* as the truth conditions of our proposition. For the conjunction "It is raining and it is sunny" ("p · q"), the series of truth conditions is *TFFF;* in other words, conjunc-

---

paraphrased as follows: "Take any selection of elementary propositions and form the conjunction of the negation of each of them; then add this proposition to the set of elementary propositions; take any selection from the enlarged set, jointly negate them, add the new proposition to the set; and continue in the same way."

tions are true when and only when both parts ["conjuncts"]
are true.

To determine the truth or falsity of such propositions,
it is not enough to consider the signs themselves; one must
find out if they agree with reality. It is for that reason that
such propositions *say* something. The proposition "It is raining or it is sunny" is false precisely when in reality it is
neither raining nor sunny.

It is different in the case of propositions having only
T's, or only *F*'s in the last column of their truth tables.
Examples are the propositions, "It is raining or it is not
raining," ("p ∨ ~ p") as well as "It is raining and it is not
raining" ("p · ~ p"). The table of truth possibilities for the
first is:

p	~p	∨
T	F	T
F	T	T

The table for the second is:

p	~p	·
T	F	F
F	T	F

In the first case we get only *T*'s for truth conditions, in the
second case only *F*'s. Wittgenstein calls propositions of the
first type tautologies, propositions of the second type, contradictions. To determine their truth or falsity, one does
not need to compare them with reality; in order to recognize that the tautology is always true and the contradiction always false, it is sufficient to consider them by themselves, thinking through their truth possibilities.
Wittgenstein describes the relationship between the various propositional types in 4.463:

> The truth conditions determine the latitude granted to the
> facts by the proposition.
>
> (The proposition, picture, or model are, in the negative
> sense, like a solid body that limits the free movement of the
> others; in the positive sense, like the space bounded by solid
> substance in which there is room for a body.)

The tautology grants to reality the whole, unlimited, logical space; the contradiction fills the whole of logical space, leaving not a point for reality. Neither can therefore determine reality in any way.

Tautology and contradiction are rather like limiting cases of propositions; that is, they are actually not propositions at all, in that they say nothing—are not pictures. They just show something:

> 4.461. The proposition shows what it says, the tautology and the contradiction show that they say nothing.
>
> The tautology has no truth conditions, for it is true unconditionally; the contradiction is under no condition true.
>
> Tautology and contradiction lack sense.
>
> (Like the point from which two arrows point in opposite directions.)

Tautology and contradiction have no sense because their truth conditions in no way determine reality. Real propositions, on the other hand, show their sense; they *show* how things stand if they are true, and they *say* that things do stand in that way (4.022). There is an important distinction, then, between, on the one hand, propositions, and, on the other hand, tautologies and contradictions; important also is the associated distinction between *saying* and *showing*. These distinctions are so important to Wittgenstein that he declares them to be the main point of the *Tractatus*. How is this so? A part of the answer lies in the fact that the propositions of "a comprehensive, world-reflecting" logic (5.511) are tautologies (6.1). That is, their general validity is not accidental but essential (6.1231f.), for it can be seen from the sign of the logical proposition alone, without regard for empirical reality, that the column of the truth conditions contain only *T*'s. (Logic could certainly just as well be constructed with contradictions [6.1202].) That propositions in particular combinations form tautologies (or contradictions) shows something about the structure of language and thereby about the logic of pictorial form. But since logic shows itself, it cannot be rendered in words—according to the basic principle "Whatever *can* be shown *cannot* be stated" (4.1212). Only the application of an adequate notation can reveal anything about the nature of the logical—it cannot be described.

Varied each time, this conception appears at several points in the *Tractatus*. It seems to be connected with the work's "fundamental idea," that the logic of facts cannot be represented. For in order "to be able to represent logical form, we would have to be able to establish ourselves with propositions outside logic, that is outside the world" (4.12). Wittgenstein draws the following conclusion at 6.124:

> The propositions of logic describe—or, better, represent—the framework of the world. They do not "treat of" anything. They presuppose that names have meaning and that elementary propositions have sense; this is their connection with the world. The fact that certain combinations of symbols—combinations possessing an essentially determinate character—are tautologies must clearly indicate something about the world. Herein lies the decisive point. We said that much is arbitrary in the symbols that we use and much is not. In logic it is only the latter [the nonarbitrary] that expresses.[47] But that means: in logic *we* do not express what we want to with the help of signs, rather the nature of the natural and necessary signs speaks for itself. . . .

Limits

In addition to the part it plays in Wittgenstein's account of the sense of the proposition and the logic of depiction, the distinction between saying and showing has a

---

47. [This note concerns the interpretation of ". . . manches an den Symbolen, die wir gebrauchen, wäre willkürlich, manches nicht. In der Logik drückt nur dieses aus: . . ."] Here the colon does not refer to what is coming; it is to be read like a semicolon. The preceding "dieses" [which we translated "the latter"] is therefore reflexive and stands for "das, was nicht willkürlich ist" [that which is not arbitrary].

more surprising and less adequately discussed role—one related to the concluding ideas of the *Tractatus*. Wittgenstein recalled this role in a letter he wrote to Ficker in October or November of 1919:

> . . . the sense of the book is an ethical one. At one time I wanted to put a sentence into the preface, which in fact is not in it, but which I will write for you now, hoping it will serve for you as a kind of key. I wanted, in fact, to write that my work consists of two parts: that presented here, and all that I have not written. And it is the second part that is really important. The ethical is, as it were, delineated by my book from the inside. And I am convinced that is the *only* way it can be *strictly* delineated.

The ethical is in fact mentioned only by way of suggestion in the *Tractatus*. The main theme is that "there can also be no ethical propositions" (6.42), that is, that there can be no true-or-false propositions ("propositions with sense") about ethical matters. (The propositions in the *Tractatus* suggesting something about the ethical realm are "pseudo-propositions" without sense.) Wittgenstein refers to ethics as "transcendental." It is unclear whether he means this in a Kantian sense having to do with "conditions of possibility," or in the sense of "transcendent," that is, "outside the realm of what can be said." Although both are possible, the first would presuppose a much more speculative interpretation than the second. A parallel passage in the *Notebooks* says "Ethics is transcendent"; it *could* be that the difference between this and the *Tractatus* indicates a development, either in conception or precision of wording. In any case, it is important that the *Tractatus* also states that "logic is transcendental" (6.13). And it is not only that logic belongs to the realm of the unsayable but also that it is a condition of the possibility of saying anything by means of language.

Implicit in the remaining ideas of the *Tractatus* is the idea that there can be no genuine (true or false) propositions in ethics. For the foundation of value cannot be compared with reality and found to be true or false. The ethical relevance of an utterance can only *show* itself.

Wittgenstein's determination that meaningful propositions must be of a certain kind shows that real value
cannot lie *in* the world, thereby throwing *indirect* light on
the ethical. It remains, however, that there can be no doctrine of value, or indeed any sensible statement about real
value.

That value is not *in* the world is connected in the way
indicated with the theory of propositional sense and the
distinction between saying and showing. It is important
for a better understanding of this idea to bear in mind
certain special aspects of Wittgenstein's notion of "the
world." In a *Notebooks* passage dated August 2, 1916, he
wrote:

> The world is then, in itself, neither good nor evil.
>
> For it must not matter, for the existence of ethics, whether
> there is life in the world or not. And it is clear that a world
> in which there is only dead matter is neither good nor evil;
> therefore, the world of living beings can in itself be neither
> good nor evil.
>
> Good and evil enter only through the *subject*. And the
> subject does not belong to the world, rather it is a boundary
> [limit] of the world.

In this passage the world is first seen as something independent—possibly dead or without subjectivity. Then,
through the presence of a subject, a boundary is drawn
and the world comes to have a certain gestalt. The subject
meant here is not the desiring subject, for the world is of
course "independent of my will" (6.373). The talk of boundaries and the comparison with seeing (5.633f.) are revealing, for "nothing about the visual field leads to the conclusion that it is seen by an eye" (5.633). Although my visual
field certainly is influenced by the fact that it is seen from
my point of view, the visual field in itself points neither to
my own viewpoint nor to that of others. My visual field is
of course inherently mine—it is impossible for me to share
it with others. But because here there is in a certain sense
no "my" and "your," I can just as well speak of *the* visual
field. Identifying the owner is "logically" superfluous. (Analo-

gously, I say that I feel pain, not that I feel *my* pain; in the area of feeling there is no my/ your contrast.)

The case of language and world is similar to that of eye and visual field. "5.6. *The limits of my language* signify the limits of my world." My world is not, however, one among many—it is not as if I could glance over from my world into yours, as one can see from the kitchen into the living room. No, *the* world is *my* world: "The world and life are one. I am my world. (The microcosm.)" (5.621f.). This appears to express a purely solipsistic position, yet the appearance is somewhat deceptive. For in order to describe the boundary that is drawn for my world by the boundary of my language, thus describing my solipsistic standpoint, I would have to go beyond both boundaries. This, however, is impossible: the boundary would not be a boundary; my world would not be mine, or a world at all; my language, not a language. "What solipsism *intends* is quite right, only it cannot be *said,* but shows itself" (5.62). Just as my visual field is my visual field, and my pain is my pain, so my world is my world. And just as I cannot get from my visual field into yours, or confuse my pain with yours, so I cannot describe my world from a standpoint lying outside of it—cannot compare it with fundamentally different possibilities. The word "my" in "my visual field" or "my pain" does not characterize *this* in contrast to *that* and can therefore, in many contexts, be dropped as superfluous. Wittgenstein draws this conclusion as follows: "5.64. Here one sees that solipsism strictly carried through coincides with pure realism. The 'I' of solipsism shrinks down to an extensionless point, and there remains the reality coordinated with it."

But what shows that solipsism is correct? That it is correct is shown through the limits (boundaries) of my language. But why *my* language? Wittgenstein cannot mean by this a language that is in any sense *private,* since he speaks throughout the *Tractatus* of understanding through propositions and of explaining the meaning of expressions. The limit of my language is just as little given by the fact that I know only a certain number of words and syntactical constructions, while my friend possesses a larger vocabulary and enjoys greater flexibility in his language than I. I draw the limit of my language through my use of language; I set a limit for language in that I use the language in a certain way. And although I cannot describe this limit, it shows itself in use: "The way a language designates things is reflected in its use" (*NB*, 9/11/16, directly after the discussion of solipsism. Cf. *TLP* 3.262 and 3.326: "That which is not expressed in the signs is shown in their use. That which signs slur over, their use makes clear./ In order to recognize the symbol in the sign, one has to pay attention to how it is used with a sense.")

I certainly draw no limit for logic by my use of language. Logic is, so to speak, the common framework of "your" and "my" language, for "all propositions of our everyday language are in perfect logical order just as they are" (5.557). Logic functions to draw a limit inasmuch as it is constantly employed in and through the use of language: "The *application* of logic determines what elementary propositions there are" (5.557). And so, the elementary propositions are not somehow "given." The application of logic, that is, my use of language, determines the elementary propositions and, in consequence, determines as well what state of affairs is available for forming the facts of my (the) world. The way I structure my language through using it determines the structure of my world.

The following [often-quoted] proposition may become clearer against this background: "That the world is *my* world can be seen from the fact that the limits of *the* language (the only language I understand) mean the limits of *my* world" (5.62). The only language I understand is the one in the use of which I connect object and name, state of affairs and elementary proposition. Thus—regardless of what signs of everyday language I use—I form propositions in accordance with a logic that others too can also understand. The use of language is, if you will, the "metaphysical subject" of 5.641. It is precisely the "unextended point" of 5.64: on one side lies communication through propositions of everyday language; on the other side lies what is "slurred over" by my use of these propositions—the structure of language proceeding from the elements of my world. Therefore it is shown in the use of language that the world is my world. Only to the extent that I successfully form propositions—and thus draw limits for my language—can I give names to objects and connect them in elementary propositions. It is *I* who use this language, *I* who name the objects, etc. That the world is thus constructed is shown in use—I cannot "say" it.

These ideas now have to be read into the beginning of the *Tractatus*. The world—everything that is the case—is essentially my world. It is life—a world that ceases with death (6.431). Its constitution can be described, while the fact of its existence can only be felt with wonder. "The facts [the constitution of the world] all contribute only to setting the problem [of existence, of life], not to its solution" (6.4321).

That which gives the world—life—value must, therefore, lie beyond the world. Understanding, with the help of the "pseudo-propositions" of the *Tractatus,* where the limits of language, world, and science lie, enables one to see the world as a limited whole. Feeling the world as a limited whole is what Wittgenstein called "mystical." He does not want to suggest, however, that those who have the feeling in question have a premonition of matters remaining hidden to others. There is no riddle here (6.5). The mystical experience is not the revelation of an arcane solution to an arcane problem.

"The mystical is not *how* the world is, but *that* it is" (6.44) recalls 5.552:

> The "experience" we need in order to understand logic is not that something is thus or so, but rather that something *is:* but that is *not* an experience.
>
> Logic is *prior* to every experience—that something is *this way.*
>
> It is prior to the how, not to the what.

"That something is" does not describe an experience in the usual sense. In the usual sense, what can be experienced can be described in meaningful sentences. Wonder or sadness or happiness about the fact of something's existence can be very real, however. While not subjects of meaningful propositions, these "experiences" can change my view of the world, and thereby my way of feeling and acting. Logic is prior to the how and, therefore, precedes everything that can be described. Logic is not prior to the what: I can only feel it as a limited whole.

Insight into limits is not something that can be communicated straight out. It is obtained only at the end of a path paved with senseless elucidations. He who has traveled this path and recognized why the elucidations are senseless is perhaps then in a position to see the world correctly, and perhaps also in a position to see it sub specie aeternitatis, that is, as a limited whole. But he must have had the experience of this path before he can "throw away the ladder" on which he ascended. And this is the kind of experience that, I think, Wittgenstein sets as a prerequisite for his readers. (See pp. 45–46.) There are all sorts of ways to come to know the limits of the sense of the world. But one must have the experience oneself; reading about it is no substitute. To realize that the *world* of the happy person is different from that of the unhappy person, even when the *facts* are precisely the same in each (6.43), is to have an experience requiring no books and no logical syntax. Yet having had this *kind* of experience may be necessary for understanding the book (cf. first sentence of the preface).

"One must be silent about that of which one cannot speak" (7): whoever has understood the *Tractatus* will understand what this, its final sentence, is getting at. "To speak" here means the same as "to make meaningful statements." Where no meaningful statements can be expressed, one should not, in Wittgenstein's view, even make the attempt to express them—as if one might just possibly succeed in making sense. Here Wittgenstein is drawing a conclusion from the "summarizing" thought of the preface, namely: "Whatever can be stated at all, can be stated clearly" (cf. 4.116). This takes to heart the motto of the book: ". . . and everything that one knows, and has not just heard blustering and making noise, can be said in three words" (Kürnberger).

Wittgenstein is not to be reproached for irrational tendencies, for he always holds to the principle that philosophy "will intimate the ineffable by clearly presenting what can be said" (4.115). He does not act as if he knew how to make the ineffable understandable. Also, philosophy can present or elucidate through paraphrase only what can be meaningfully stated; if it succeeds in fulfilling this task, it will perhaps succeed in pointing to the ineffable as that which lies outside the boundary.

3

***

Connecting Links

Much of what cannot be said but only shown, according to the doctrine of the *Tractatus*, Wittgenstein attempts to express indirectly. Although meant to cancel themselves in their entirety, the "propositions" of the *Tractatus* are still supposed to convey a message, if only a negative one. In the years of silence after the publication of his book, little at first seems to change in Wittgenstein's basic ideas. His writings, and the statements of others from the first years after his return to philosophy in 1928/29, are strongly reminiscent of the *Tractatus*—this despite the fact that he was attempting to slough off what, in the following conversation with Waismann, he termed the "dogmatism" of that work:

> First of all, one can criticize a dogmatic presentation for a certain arrogance. But even that's not the worst part. There is another, much more dangerous error, that permeates my entire book—namely, the conception that there are questions for which answers would be discovered at a later date. Although one does not have the answer, one thinks that one has the method by which an answer can be found. I for one thought that it was the task of logical analysis to discover the elementary propositions. I wrote that we are unable to specify the form of elementary propositions, and that was quite correct too. It was clear to me that there are no hypotheses here and that one cannot proceed with these questions in the way Carnap did, by assuming at the outset that elementary propositions consist of two-place relations. But I did think that one would be able to specify the elementary propositions later. . . .

What I want to oppose here is the false idea that we could
hit upon something that today we do not see, that we can
discover something entirely new. That is a mistake. In
truth, we already have everything; in fact, it is *present,* so
that we do not have to wait for anything. We move within
the realm of something already there, the grammar of our
accustomed language. Therefore, we already have
everything and need not wait for the future. (*WVC,* pp. 182–
83).

From this point on, the stress is on the meaning of the
propositional *system* as opposed to the individual proposition; the boundary between sense and nonsense is drawn
differently; the criteria for the sense of a proposition are
given a more complex formulation, and increasingly linked
to the *use* of linguistic expressions. There is, then, a plethora
of new ideas and the gradual emergence of a conception
that could not be foreseen from the standpoint of the
Tractatus. In spite of all that, it remains that the point of
these writings—the *Philosophical Remarks* and *Philosophical Grammar,* the oral statements passed on by Waismann,
Moore, Lee, Ambrose, among others—was to reconcile the
new with the old, to elaborate and illuminate the statements of the *Tractatus*. There is no question of a new
philosophy or of a radical rejection of the ideas of the
first book. Wittgenstein certainly practices self-criticism,
but it remains within the framework of the *Tractatus*
philosophy.[48]

---

48. The critique of the *Tractatus* conception begins very timidly with a
revision of the concept of the elementary proposition: "I used to have two
conceptions of an elementary proposition, one of which seems correct to me,
while I was completely wrong in holding the other. My first assumption
was this: that in analyzing propositions we must eventually reach
propositions that are immediate connections of objects without any help
from logical constants, for 'not', 'and', 'or', and 'if' [do not] connect objects.
And I still adhere to that. Secondly I had the idea that elementary
propositions must be independent of one another. A complete description
of the world would be a product of elementary propositions, as it were,
these being partly positive and partly negative. In holding this I was
wrong, and the following is what is wrong with it: I laid down rules for the
syntactical use of the logical constants, for example 'p·q', and did not think

The Ethical

The ethical is equated with the aesthetic and connected—in a way impossible to elucidate—with mystical and religious ideas. According to the conception of the *Tractatus*, it belongs in the realm of what can be shown but not said. In the strictly philosophical manuscripts of his later period, Wittgenstein hardly addresses these matters, although he continued to express himself on them in conversations, lectures, and remarks such as those collected in *Culture and Value*. This material provides ample evidence that, in the first period after his return to philosophy, Wittgenstein was developing the complex of ideas from the *Tractatus* relating to the ethical. The items making up this evidence include an outline written for a lecture on ethics in 1929 and a detailed set of notes taken by Waismann on conversations with Wittgenstein. It is striking and characteristic that these two documents relate to Wittgenstein's oral statements, and that they are not included in the philosophical writings proper.

The "Lecture on Ethics" is not an original contribution to ethics as a philosophical discipline; it is a thoroughly characteristic document of Wittgenstein's personality. The fact/value distinction is stressed just as much as it was in the *Tractatus* where it was stated that "all propositions are of equal value" (6.4). In the "Lecture" it is said that just as with facts, so with propositions: all are on the same plane. The description of a gruesome murder is no less about facts than is the description of a stroll in the park, even

---

these rules might have something to do with the inner structure of propositions. What was wrong about my conception was that I believed that the syntax of logical constants could be laid down without paying attention to the inner connection of propositions. That is not how things actually are. I cannot, for example, say that red and blue are simultaneously at one and the same point. Here no logical product can be constructed. Rather, the rules for the logical constants form only a part of a more comprehensive syntax about which I did not yet know anything at that time" (*WVC*, p. 73f). The implicit self-criticism in the lecture "Some Remarks on Logical Form" of 1929 reads similarly. On this transitional period, see Hacker, *Insight and Illusion*, chapter 4.

though the former arouses outrage and horror while the latter arouses no strong emotions. Feelings are also facts and can be described quite impartially; they can by no means be used to assign value to things to which they relate.[49] Language in its meaningful use—in science—is able to express only factual matters:

> Our words used as we use them in science, are vessels capable only of containing and conveying meaning and sense, *natural* meaning and sense. Ethics, if it is anything, is supernatural, and our words will only express facts; as a teacup will only hold a teacup full of water even if I were to pour out a gallon over it.

The "Lecture," but not the *Tractatus,* contains the distinction between the *relative* and the *absolute* (or *ethical*) use of "good" and "correct." The relative use is involved when the action's purpose fixes the (generally recognized) criteria for carrying it out "well" or "correctly." Suppose that I play the piano, and an expert judges that I do not do it well: it is open to me to answer that I have no desire to play any better. But now suppose I peddle some slanderous publication from door to door and then someone reproaches, saying that I have "behaved disgracefully": it is not open to me to answer by saying, "Of course I behaved badly, but I have no desire to behave decently." The judgment that I *ought* to behave decently is on a different level than any judgment of relative value. The difference goes back to the fact that judgments of relative value can be translated into statements of fact containing no value terms, but that such a reformulation is precluded in the case of judgments of absolute or ethical value. One consequence Wittgenstein draws from this is that there is no science of ethics. Nothing "intrinsically sublime," nothing above other subject matters could be described in a scientific book: "If a man could write a book on Ethics which really was a book

---

49. Cf. *WVC,* p. 116: "What is valuable in a Beethoven sonata? The sequence of notes? No, for it is, after all, one sequence among many. Indeed, I would even go so far as to say that the feelings Beethoven had when composing this sonata were no more valuable than any other feelings."

on Ethics, this book would, with an explosion, destroy all the other books in the world." In spite of all that, Wittgenstein does not want completely to exclude judgments of absolute value; what he wants is for us to take seriously the indicated "change of level," leaving behind whatever pertains to description, explanation, and intersubjectivity when speaking of absolute value:

> If someone gives me a *theory,* I would say "No, no! That does not interest me." Even if the theory were true, it would not interest me—for *that* would never be the object of my search.
>
> The ethical cannot be taught. If it took a theory to explain the nature of the ethical to someone, then the ethical would have no value at all.
>
> At the conclusion of my lecture on ethics I spoke in the first person. That, I believe, is something very important. Here nothing further can be substantiated. I can only step forth as an individual and speak in the first person.
>
> *For me* theory has no value. A theory gives me nothing. (*WVC,* pp. 116–17).

I have to "speak in the first person" about what seems to me to have absolute value. In line with this, Wittgenstein proceeds to describe certain experiences of his own that have absolute value for him—although the "descriptions" he employs are necessarily allusive and metaphorical. He characterizes the first experience as amazement that there is a world—amazement that anything at all exists.[50] The second experience is one of complete confidence—the feeling that "I am safe *whatever* happens."[51] The linguistic

---

50. Cf. *TLP* 6.44: "The mystical is not *how* the world is, but rather *that* it is."

51. Presumably Wittgenstein actually had an experience of this kind in connection with a performance of Ludwig Anzengruber's "The Cross Makers." It is in the decisive scene of that play that the proverbial line "Nothing can happen to me!" occurs. Cf. McGuinness, "The Mysticism of Wittgenstein's *Tractatus*" and *Wittgenstein: A Life*, Vol. I, chapter 4, p. 94; Malcolm, *Memoir*, p. 58.

expression of these experiences is, strictly speaking, meaningless, however. I may be amazed that the world is made
this way rather than that, thus and not otherwise. But
what is it to be amazed that anything at all exists?—that
would be like being surprised at the tautology "The sky is
either blue or not blue."[52] Equally senseless is the statement that I am absolutely safe no matter what might happen. For to speak of being safe is meaningful only where
there is a corresponding situation of uncertainty or danger.
But "absolute" certainty is supposed to exclude precisely
that contrasting situation. Then what is "certainty" supposed to mean? The obvious response to this challenge—
suggesting that the idiom in which these experiences are
described is figurative—actually leads nowhere. For if something can be expressed in an image or figure, it also can be
expressed objectively.[53] Wittgenstein's view is that we simply have to acknowledge the paradox in the situation he
describes. An experience is a fact, and a fact cannot contain any absolute, supernatural value. Yet the experiences
mentioned are for him—from his personal ("first-person")
standpoint—examples of the ethical, the absolute. He
says that some people will respond to his examples and
know what he is getting at, while others will prefer to
appeal to quite different experience, or perhaps to religious scriptures.

The scientific explicability or inexplicability of the experience in question is not the issue here. The most amazing "miracle" can be examined from a scientific point of
view, but as soon as it is examined in this way it loses its
miraculous character, regardless of whether one can explain it or not. On the other hand, common, uncomplicated,
inconspicuous things can acquire a meaning if viewed in a

---

52. Cf. *TLP* 5.552: "The 'experience' that we need in order to understand
logic is not that something is thus or so, but rather that something *is:* but
that is *not* an experience./ Logic is *prior* to every experience—that something
is this way./ It is prior to the how, not to the what."

53. Cf. *WVC,* p. 117: "Religious speech is not metaphorical either; for
otherwise one would have to be able to say the same thing in prose."

certain way—a meaning that can be communicated even though not open to sensible rendering in factual language. An example is "Count Eberhards's Hawthorne," a poem by [Ludwig] Uhland that Wittgenstein admired, and wrote about in a letter to Englemann dated April 9, 1917. "If one makes no attempt to express the inexpressible," he wrote, "then *nothing* is lost, but the inexpressible is—inexpressibly—*contained* in what is expressed!"

Wittgenstein says that we have to come to terms with the fact that the miraculous, the religious, and indeed everything that appears really valuable to us, eludes meaningful expression in the sensible language that is the only one suited for science. He is not saying that science is base, nor is he saying that all *personal* attempts to express what is of absolute or ethical value have to be rejected as nonsense. We are dealing here with two fundamentally different levels; there is no middle level where the speech is simultaneously scientific and (in the strict sense) ethical:

> Ethics so far as it springs from the desire to say something about the ultimate meaning of life, the absolute good, the absolute valuable, can be no science. What it says does not add to our knowledge in any sense.[54]

We can say in advance of experience that the attempt to put the ethical into words is doomed to failure. "Running up against the limits of language" is how Wittgenstein characterizes this attempt, and he mentions Kierkegaard in connection with it.[55] This running up against the limits of language constitutes ethics, according to Wittgenstein. And although he regards it as completely futile, he also regards it as manifesting a "drive" of mankind that he, for his part, respects deeply and would not ridicule for anything:

---

54. "Lecture on Ethics," conclusion.

55. On Wittgenstein's attitude toward Kierkegaard, see Drury's "Some Notes on Conversations," especially pp. 102–04. In earlier years Wittgenstein was evidently an admirer of Kierkegaard, referring to him as

But the tendency, the running up against something, *indicates something.* St. Augustine knew this when he said: "What, you filthy beast, you don't want to talk nonsense? Go ahead, talk nonsense! It makes no difference." (*WVC*, p. 69).

The Magical

That the objective, factual language of science stands on another level than the sphere of absolute values is a constant in Wittgenstein's thinking. Thus in the "Lectures on Religious Belief" from the late thirties (when part of the *Investigations* already was written), Wittgenstein keeps emphasizing that words such as "proof," "reason," and "probability" in religious expressions or discussions play an entirely different role than they do in scientific presentations or discussions and are used in a completely different sense. Not even the concept of truth can have the same function as in scientifically oriented language:

> The historical reports of the Gospels could be manifestly false in the historical sense, and yet belief lose nothing by this: but *not* because it appealed to "universal truths of reason." Rather, because the historical proof (the historical proof-game) has nothing at all to do with belief. . . . A believer's relationship to these reports is *neither* that of a person to historical truth (probability) *nor* that of a person to a teaching of "truths of reason." (1937, *CV*, p. 32).

The absolute separation of the level of values from the level of the scientifically (objectively) describable is charac-

---

"by far the deepest thinker of the preceding century"; in later years he believed Kierkegaard to be "too prolix":

> . . . he says the same thing again and again. As I read his material, I always want to say: "All right, I am completely of your opinion, but please get on with it'."

Not to be excluded is the possibility that Drury's own very positive attitude towards Kierkegaard has somewhat colored his representation.

teristic of Wittgenstein. Also characteristic is the way he connects the difference in levels with a difference in practical conduct. In the previously introduced remark, therefore, he denies that the "game"—the context of action where historical proofs are employed—has anything to do with belief. Thus historians, to the extent they espouse "absolute" convictions, will not allow themselves to be impressed one way or the other by the presence or the absence of historical proof in the area of religious belief—even though they accept nothing in their field that is not appropriately authenticated by the methods of their discipline. Statements that have the same outward grammatical form are *treated* differently, according to the context. This also means that language used in the context of actions defined by absolute values functions differently than does language used in scientific investigation.

Take the word "proof." Its meaning in criminology is similar to its meaning in physics or art history. (Or perhaps we should say that it has several slightly different but closely related meanings.) One reason for this is that the proofs are similarly dealt with, have similar significance, and are highly valued in all of these areas. In all areas accessible to objective language, if a conviction is proven false, its contradictory is accepted as true; if the defendant is shown to be innocent, then the hypothesis of his guilt is rejected as false, and he is released. By contrast, questions about the truth or falsity of reports in the Gospels play no role in belief. To the extent that the words "proof," "true," and "false," are used here at all, their use is quite different from that in the context just mentioned. The meaning of the Gospels for my life—whether I experience repentance in certain circumstances, feel relief after confession, etc.—can be very closely connected with the contents of these reports. Because, however, there is no need for concern with their veracity or falsity, they are not reports in the same sense as are those of police officers or natural scientists.

The whole function of language is different in the area of absolute values from what it is in the area of scientific statements. For example, "When speaking goes on in religion, that is itself a component of religious behavior and not a theory. It is therefore not a question of whether the words are true, false, or nonsensical" (*WVC*, p. 117). Although this view may be theologically contestable, philosophically it points ahead to fundamental ideas of Wittgenstein's mature view, stressing as it does that linguistic meaning cannot be conceived independent of learned, institutionalized contexts of action.

This theme is pertinently dealt with in the "Remarks on Frazer's *The Golden Bough*," which come mainly from the early thirties. Wittgenstein again and again insists that Frazer goes wrong in presenting the rituals and magical practices of other cultures as if they were based on pseudoscientific theories. If they were so based, we would be able to see nothing profound, dark, or uncanny in them. They would be nothing more than mistakes we no longer make or have discarded. If we came across a tribe with such customs, we would have to be able to persuade them to give up their *erroneous* practice:

> It can, and frequently does, happen today that a person gives up a practice after recognizing an error on which it is based. But this happens only where making the person aware of his error is enough to dissuade him from his behavior. It does not happen where the religious customs of a people are concerned, and *therefore* there is *no* question of error in that case. (*RF*, p. 62).

A fundamental difference exists between being confronted with behavior having the status of a magical or religious procedure, and being confronted with behavior having the status of a practice grounded in science or experience. This difference is expressed in various ways, for example in whether or not we introduce proofs and reasons, refer to documents and reports of witnesses, and speak of truth and error, or probability and confirmation. The connection between institutionalized behavior and language becomes particularly clear in this context, for the same words are assigned totally different values in different fields. Suppose, for example, that a certain torchlight procession is based on the legend of a saint. The proposition, "The saint walked to the cathedral after three days of fasting, with the torch in his hand," may keep its meaning for those who sympathetically follow the torchlight procession, even if historians irrefutably prove that the proposition is false. The meaning—radiance, weight—of such a proposition is often quite independent of whether it is true or false.

Another side of the connection between language and ritualistic or magical actions is revealed in the fact that such actions sometime imitate linguistic functions:

> To burn in effigy. To kiss the picture of one's beloved. These are *of course not* based on the belief in a certain effect on the object represented by the picture.
>
> ... One could also kiss the name of the beloved, and here the representation through a name comes out clearly. (*RF*, p. 64).

It also happens that linguistic elements of this kind are woven into ritualistic actions, so that language and action are in a sort of mirroring relationship:

> In the old rituals we find the use of an extremely well-developed language of gestures.
>
> And when I read Frazer, I want to say in every instance: All of these processes, all of these changes of meaning, are still present in our word language. If "the Corn Wolf" is the name given not only to what conceals itself in the last sheaf, but also to the sheaf itself, and to the person who ties it, then we recognize here a well-known linguistic process. (*RF*, pp. 70–71).

From the example of linkage and mirroring of linguistic and magical/religious processes, one can gain insight into a more general connection between language and action. This is because "There is a whole mythology in our language" (*RF*, p. 70), and a mythology stands in an entirely different relationship to action than does a theory.[56]

---

56. In his last notes Wittgenstein wrote that the sentences describing our *world picture* could be thought of as a kind of *mythology* (*OC*, § 95). Cf. chapter 6, section 2 of this text.

Overview

Again and again Wittgenstein criticizes authors who, like Frazer, interpret the customs of foreign cultures as though they rested on beliefs in the manner of scientific theories. He is equally opposed to the widespread tendency to represent the scientific method of explanation as the only useful or acceptable method. He gives an abbreviated version of this conviction in the demand: "We must do away with all explanation and allow only description in its place" (*PI*, § 109). Explanations are viewed very negatively, characteristic of his later writings in general and of the *Philosophical Investigations* in particular. (Wittgenstein has scientific-theoretical explanations in mind here; he does not object to "explanations" in the sense of clarifications of meaning.)

With regard to representations of practices of foreign cultures, Wittgenstein writes that "the historical explanation, the explanation as hypothesis of development" is

> . . . just one way of summarizing—or giving a synopsis—of the data. It is possible to see the data in their relationships to each other, and to summarize them in a general picture, without resorting to an hypothesis of temporal development. (*RF*, p. 69).

The crucial thing, according to Wittgenstein, is to summarize the data in a way that enables us to gain insight and understanding. In order to make knowledge or understanding possible, it is not necessary for explanations to follow always the same—"hypothetico-deductive" or axiomatic—pattern.

"And so the chorus indicates a secret law." Thus quoting Goethe, Wittgenstein develops in the briefest way the method of his later philosophy. While discussing customs described by Frazer in the same passage, he writes:

> This law, this idea, I *can* present through an hypothesis of development, or also, analogously to the scheme of a plant [as in Goethe's theory of plants], by means of the schema of

a religious ceremony, or by just arranging the factual material in a *"clearly arranged"* presentation.

"Clearly arranged presentation" [*übersichtliche Darstellung*] is one of Wittgenstein's most important concepts. In criticizing other authors, he frequently deplores the lack of clarity in the arrangement of what they present. This is especially true in his remarks on proofs in mathematics. While not especially emphasizing either the rigor of the inferences or the evidence of the premises, he persistently stresses the importance of clarity.

Many may be surprised at the mention of Spengler in this connection. But, as with the quotation from Goethe, the reference to Spengler points the way to a more specific interpretation of the idea of a clearly arranged presentation. "This concept," writes Wittgenstein:

> . . . is of fundamental importance for us. It characterizes the form or our presentation, the way we see things. (A variant of the apparently typical "weltanschauung" of our times. Spengler.)

It is characteristic that the much later version of this thought in the *Philosophical Investigations* (§ 122) reduces the parenthetical remark to: "(Is this a "weltanschauung"?)." Spengler's name, as well as the Goethe quotation and the allusion to a "schematic plant," make it clear that Wittgenstein is thinking of a "morphological" interpretation in Goethe's sense.[57] The simple, basic idea of morphology is that of a representation that links together the phenomena to be explained in a continuous series, a representation that can be taken in at a glance. The phenomena are arranged as clearly indicated steps of a stepladder free of gaps. As Wittgenstein often formulates it, this

---

57. Spengler subtitles *Decline of the West* "Outline of a Morphology of World History" and refers expressly to Goethe's scientific writings. Cf. Haller, "Was Wittgenstein Influenced by Spengler?," as well as Schulte, "Chor und Gesetz. Zur 'morphologischen Methode' bei Goethe und Wittgenstein."

idea requires that the rendering of the objects in question, or the proof, present a "gestalt," "face," or "physiognomy."

If for no other reason than the inexactness of expressions such as "all steps" and "with no gaps," such a method of explanation can never satisfy the strict requirements of an exact science. Nor is that its goal. What *is* essential is that connections be presented in a continuum. If one step is missing, we have to find it, for otherwise we do not yet have a clear view of things. Understanding provides an overview "by allowing us to 'see connections.' Hence the importance of finding *connecting links.*" It is significant that in a later version of this remark (*PI*, § 122), Wittgenstein spoke of inventing, as well as of finding, these connecting links ["intermediate cases," in some translations]. Already in the version written in 1931, he spoke of "hypothetical"—thus invented—connecting links:

> A hypothetical connecting link should in this case do nothing but direct attention to the similarity, the connection, of the *facts.* An internal relation between the form of a circle and that of an ellipse is illustrated by gradually changing an ellipse into a circle. *But this is done not to establish that a certain ellipse is in fact historically derived from a circle* (developmental hypothesis), but only to sharpen our perception of the formal connection.

This remark relates, of course, to the representation of actually exiting practices. However, philosophers do not have to rely absolutely on facts when explaining, or trying to prevent confusion about, the concepts we actually employ. "We are not engaged in natural science; neither are we engaged in natural history—for we can, of course, fabricate natural history for our purposes" (*PI*, Part II, § xii).

Grammar

The frequent use of the words "grammar" and "grammatical" is characteristic of Wittgenstein's later philosophy generally and of the writings from the '30s in particular.

But these words are used in two senses. Wittgenstein often speaks of the grammar of a certain word or phrase—for example: "to fit," "to be able," "to understand" (*PI*, § 182); "to know," "to opine" (*PI*, § 187). In these cases it appears that "grammar" is supposed to mean "the way these words or phrases are used"; here the discussion is about fine distinctions in the rules of usage. In other places, "grammar" seems to refer to the totality of the rules of a language or a language-fragment—as in the remark: "Grammar does not say how a language has to be constructed in order to fulfil its purpose, in order to have such and such an effect on people. It only describes, but never in any way explains, the use of signs" (*PI*, § 496).

These apparently very different uses of the words "grammar" and "grammatical" are connected by the fundamental idea of the later philosophy, that linguistic meaning is essentially the *use* of expressions. The sort of systems of rules he talks about are not independent of use—they have application either in real or in coherently imaginable situations.

In a sense, the concept of grammar in the later writings is the successor of the concept of logic in the early writings. "Logic has to take care of itself" (*NB*, 8/22/14); thus reads the first sentence of the extant diaries. Wittgenstein continues by emphasizing the independence of logic from facts:

> A *possible* sign must be able to signify. Everything that is at all possible is also legitimate (permitted). Let us remember the explanation of why 'Socrates is Plato' is nonsense. It is nonsense because *we* have not made an arbitrary specification, NOT because the sign is in and of itself somehow illegitimate.[58]

And the following passage from notes on a 1931 lecture is reminiscent of the *Tractatus* in its choice of words and its characterization of the "calculus" of language:

---

58. Cf. the parallel passage in *TLP* 5.473. Note the revealing textual differences between the earlier and the latter version.

> The place of a word in logical space fixed by grammar *is* its
> meaning. You cannot say that in order that a word should
> be used as it is it must have *these* rules. The meaning of a
> word is given if you describe language by all its rules. All
> explanations take place *inside* language. They would only
> transcend language if they made assertions of fact, which
> they do not. The meanings of the words are part of language.
> (*WLL,* pp. 61–62).

For Wittgenstein in the early '30s, language is a kind of
calculus, a system determined throughout by exceptionless
rules. But the reason he gave in support of this "calculus
view" contained a seed of the later "language-game" conception, as well as the reason for abandoning the calculus
model itself: "Language is for us a calculus; it is characterized by *linguistic activities*" (*PG*, p. 193).

Wittgenstein thought that rules of grammar formed a
total system: A system that can, in principle, be reconstructed. A system that, completely presented, would remove the problems of philosophy—for then there would be
nothing left to explain. He claimed to be speaking of grammar in the strict sense only when he actually was able to
explain the rules:

> Can one then also speak of a grammar when someone is
> taught language purely through training? Clearly, I could
> use the word "grammar" only in a degenerate sense if I used
> it in such a case: for then I could speak of "explanation" or
> "agreement" only in a degenerate sense. (*PG,* p. 191).[59]

Although in later writings Wittgenstein certainly will not
maintain that explicitly formulated (or formulable) rules
do (or should) play no role in learning language or solving
philosophical problems, he will emphasize the role of tactily

---

59. Wittgenstein continues: "A trained child or animal is not acquainted
with any problems of philosophy." In his later writings Wittgenstein no
longer wants explicit explanations. To put his later view perhaps a bit too
pointedly: Those tormented by philosophical problems are released from
them when persuaded to see themselves as basically nothing but "trained
children or animals."

learned rules, making it clear that rules learned in this way are not a whit less valuable than those learned explicitly. He speaks of "agreement" in the passage just quoted, seeming to insinuate that linguistic rules are, or should be, conceived as explicitly learned conventions. And he says in one place, straight out, that "grammar consists of agreements" (*PG,* p. 190).[60] Grammatical rules are conventions to the extent that they cannot be justified by proving that "a representation made in agreement with them agrees with reality. For this justification would itself have to describe that which is represented" (*PG,* p. 186). Therefore grammar—like the "logic" of the early writings—is completely independent of the facts. Can it, then, be said about grammar as it was about logic that its employment is a matter of "arbitrary specification"? Apparently so. "Grammar is not beholden to any reality. The grammatical rules are what determine the meaning—constitute it; they are, therefore, not answerable to any meaning and are, to that extent, arbitrary" (*PG,* p. 184).

The *Philosophical Investigations* puts the matter much more carefully when it says that one can "call the rules of grammar 'arbitrary' if one means thereby that the *purpose* of grammar is only that of the language" (§ 497). Still, this more cautious formulation rests on considerations proposed in the '30s and illustrated by means of the following comparison:

> Why do I not call the rules of cooking arbitrary? And why am I tempted to call the rules of grammar arbitrary? Because I think that the concept "cooking" is defined by the purpose of cooking, but that the concept "language" is not defined by the purpose of language. Whoever cooks according to rules other than the proper ones for cooking, cooks poorly. But whoever follows rules other than those for chess plays another game; and whoever follows grammatical rules other than the customary ones, is not therefore saying something wrong, but rather speaking of something else. (*PG,* p. 184f.).

---

60. Cf. *PI,* § 355: "(And this language rests, like any other, on convention.)"

It is certainly surprising that here Wittgenstein takes it as a matter of course that someone speaking a language determined by "other rules" must not only be playing a different game but also referring to other states of affairs—for the words "speaking of something else" must indeed be interpreted in this way. But, aside from this peculiarity, Wittgenstein articulates an especially important insight in this passage: the insight that language cannot be defined by a purpose external to it. To be sure, one can do all sorts of things with language—which makes it useful for various purposes. However, none of these purposes determines the nature of language—not even if "the purpose" is formulated in some such general way as "understanding" or "expression of thought."

Wittgenstein's admittedly fluctuating concept of grammar also is tied to thoughts of the *Tractatus* period through the notion of a "grammatical proposition." In the *Tractatus* Wittgenstein speaks of "pseudo-propositions" that are "nonsensical" because, rather than symbolizing formal concepts ("object," "proposition," "number," etc.) with variables (as they should), they treat them as if they were "actual" concept-words (Cf. *TLP* 4.126ff.). He, of course, constantly uses such pseudo-propositions himself. For despite their nonsensicality—or because of it—they indirectly facilitate certain insights.

Only in a few quite special cases do grammatical propositions have a function—for example, in teaching a language or in warning about misuses of language that occur in doing philosophy—as when one reads substantive content into a proposition that is either self-evident in virtue of customary usage or functioning to explicate a concept. Wittgenstein offers the following examples of grammatical propositions: "My thoughts are private"; "Only I can know if I'm feeling pain"; "Every stick has a length" (*PI*, § 251); "An order orders its own execution" (*PI*, § 458); and "The class of lions is not a lion, but the class of classes is a class" (*RFM*, Part VII, § 36).

Grammatical propositions have no function in most language games, and they can be misleading because of their formal similarity to more common propositions. They are not, in reality, part of any verification/falsification game. If I say, "This garden is private," one knows how to verify it; its contradiction is not only thinkable but quite possibly true. But if I say "My feelings are private," then the thought of a possible contradiction does not even arise, for the assertion contains no factually related information about my feelings; at most it can teach the hearer something about the use of the word "feeling" or remind him of it. Because it remains completely on the linguistic level, the proposition is outside the dimension of truth and falsity. Using an expression Wittgenstein applied to tautologies in *Remarks on the Foundations of Mathematics* (Part III, § 33), one could characterize grammatical propositions as "degenerate propositions on the side of truth."

Foundations and Contradictions

Problems in the foundations of mathematics were a recurrent interest of Wittgenstein's. Already in 1909 he formulated an analysis of Russell's paradox, and during the early years at Cambridge his major work was on logic and mathematics.

There is a very concise presentation of his thoughts on mathematics in *Tractatus* 6.2ff. According to that, mathematics is basically equations, and equations are "pseudo-propositions." An equation does not express a thought; it brings together expressions and characterizes a standpoint from which they are to be viewed. Mathematics is a logical method: ". . . in life it is never the mathematical proposition that we want, rather we use the mathematical proposition *only* in order to make inferences from propositions not belonging to mathematics to propositions which also do not belong to mathematics" (6.211).[61]

As we have seen, Wittgenstein's return to philosophy was in part occasioned by his reflection on ideas that

---

61. Anticipating later thoughts, he adds: "(In philosophy the question, 'What do we actually use this word or this proposition for?' repeatedly leads to valuable insights.)"

Brouwer had presented in a lecture in Vienna. The constructivist element in Brouwer's intuitionism appealed to Wittgenstein as did the formalism of David Hilbert and his school. Accordingly, Wittgenstein said in a conversation with Schlick and Waismann that Frege did not

> . . . see what is justified in formalism, namely that mathematical symbols are signs but lack meaning. For Frege the alternatives were as follows: either we are dealing with ink marks on paper, or else these ink marks are signs of *something,* and what they stand in for is their meaning. That these alternatives are not exhaustive can be seen in the game of chess. Although we are not here concerned with the wooden figures, these figures do not stand in for anything; they have no meaning in Frege's sense. There is still a third alternative: the signs can be used as in a game. (*WVC,* p. 105).

However, Wittgenstein himself did not take sides in the allegedly fundamental issue between formalists, logicists, intuitionists, and platonists.[62] He understood the task of the philosopher not as that of contributing to mathematical research, but as that of coming to an understanding of the specifically philosophical questions that can be raised through mathematics. Therefore, in section 124 of *Philosophical Investigations,* where he insists that philosophy leaves everything the way it is, Wittgenstein adds: "It also leaves mathematics as it is, and no mathematical discovery can bring it any further." Of course, he does not want to deny that one and the same person can be doing mathematics and philosophy; he wants to say that mathematics and philosophy are completely separate activities. He sees the philosophical debate about foundations as an interrup-

---

62. At a 1930 congress in Königsberg, Waismann indeed presented a lecture "On the Essence of Mathematics: The Standpoint of Wittgenstein." This setting—where Carnap gave a paper on logistic, Heyting on intuitionism, and von Neumann on formalism—could have created the impression that Wittgenstein took a distinctive position of his own, one fundamentally opposed to the others. Cf. *WVC,* pp. 102f. What was preserved of Waismann's lecture is reprinted in his book, *Lectures on the Philosophy of Mathematics,* pp. 157–67.

tion: once past this interruption, mathematics will be able to do without the various ideas involved in that debate. "Once the conflict about its foundations is over, I believe that mathematics will look again as it does in elementary school, where the abacus is used" (*WVC*, p. 105f.).

In Wittgenstein's opinion, the peace of mathematics is disturbed by demands for consistency proofs—demands such as the following from Hilbert:

> . . . a satisfactory conclusion of the investigations of these fundamentals [can] be reached only by solving the problem of the consistency of the axioms of analysis. If we succeed in this proof, then we will have established that mathematical pronouncements are indeed unassailable and definitive truths—a point that is of the greatest importance for us because of its general philosophical character.[63]

Wittgenstein raises several objections to the attitude expressed in this demand, objections that are of special interest because of the connection they reveal between his thoughts on mathematics and his "verificationist" conception of sense or meaning.

He develops his basic verificationist ideas in connection with "seeking and finding." The activity of seeking in mathematics is fundamentally different from the activity of seeking a material object. The way I seek a material object, and the possible places I look for it, are in principle unlimited. But in mathematics, the calculus prescribes where I am to seek, and the techniques of search are more or less determined. A compass and straightedge are not suitable instruments for solving a problem in addition. I know what I am looking for in mathematics only when I know a technique and procedure for finding it. The situation is similar in other areas. To state the matter with some exaggeration: ". . . it is only the method of answering a question that teaches you what the question was actually about. I cannot know what I have asked until I have

---

63. Hilbert, "Neubegrundung der Mathematik," p. 162.

answered the question. (The sense of a proposition is the
method of its verification.)" (*WVC,* p. 79).

Should we come up against contradictions in mathematics, we must do something—for example, make new
arrangements to prevent them in the future. However, when
we talk of looking for a contradiction in mathematics, we
really have no idea what we are looking for; our "question"
lacks sense because it is not connected with any known
technique of seeking. Where no verification procedure is
known, our utterances have no sense and we have no idea
what is actually going on. One tends to confuse seeking
and finding in mathematics—which is basically calculation, according to Wittgenstein—with the seeking and discovery that takes place in nature: "One imagines that there
could be a contradiction that no one has ever seen hidden
in the axioms from the beginning, like tuberculosis. Suspecting nothing, one suddenly drops dead. And so it is
thought, by analogy, that a hidden contradiction could erupt
and bring catastrophe" (*WVC,* p. 120).

Nearly ten years after the conversation with Schlick
and Waismann from which we have been quoting,
Wittgenstein discussed similar problems with Turing and
others. Again he complains about the view that one must
always be on guard against *hidden* contradictions and that
one cannot trust one's calculation so long as it has not
been proven free of contradiction. Turing objected that the
fear of hidden contradiction is justified inasmuch as a
calculus permitting contradictory calculations could have
fatal practical results. He also objected that a system permitting derivation of the contradiction "p · ~ p" is of no
use, inasmuch as any arbitrary conclusion can be drawn
from it. These objections are not without justification.
Wittgenstein had to make concessions to them in the course
of the discussion, repeatedly retreating to precarious distinctions between possible uses of mathematical rules and
procedures (*LFM,* pp. 209–26). Where seeking a contradiction can be based on certain techniques, Wittgenstein has
no convincing reason for opposing the desire for a consistency proof. What bothers him, in essence, is the *attitude*
of those who speak of not being able to trust computations

in the absence of a consistency proof. Absolute certainty—
the protection against every possible mistake—cannot be
required, even in mathematics. Thus:

> One can even imagine a savage's having been given Frege's
> logic as an instrument with which to derive arithmetical
> propositions. He derives a contradiction without noticing
> that it is a contradiction, and from that he now derives
> arbitrary true and false propositions.
>
> [Interlocutor:] "Till now a guardian angel has protected us
> from taking *this* path." [Wittgenstein:] Well, what else do
> you want? I think one could say: "You'll always need a
> guardian angel, whatever you do." (*RFM*, Part VII, § 16).

The Hardness of the Logical Must

"With a full philosophical rucksack, I can only climb
the mountain of mathematics slowly" (*CV*, p. 2). This, from
a 1929 notebook, implies that there is something for the
philosopher to do in mathematics; the following, from *Remarks on the Foundations of Mathematics,* implies that
the philosopher would be ill-advised to work from a traditional "foundations problematic":

> Why the need to lay foundations for mathematics?
> Foundations are needed for mathematics as little, I think,
> as *analysis* is needed for propositions dealing with physical
> objects, or with sense impressions. To be sure, mathematical
> propositions as well as those other propositions need
> clarification of their grammar.
>
> *Mathematical* "foundations" problems are for us just as
> little at the foundations of mathematics as the painted
> rocks are at the foundations of the painted mountain. (Part
> VII, § 16).

Instead of getting involved in the traditional arguments,
Wittgenstein makes comparisons—between laboratory ex-
periment and mathematical calculation, for instance.
Through one new example after another, he emphasizes

how important it is for a proof to have a "face" or "physiognomy"—to be organized in such a way that it can be easily followed. He frequently invents situations intended to depict possible alien contexts for our mathematical techniques. In doing that, he is not arguing that mathematics and its techniques depend on the purposes set by society. They may, indeed, be just a game, with no purposes at all. Yet even a pure game requires a context, for only in a context are there customs, practices, and institutions. It is "the motley of mathematics" that Wittgenstein is most of all concerned to bring out. "Mathematics is a MOTLEY of techniques of proof" (*RFM,* Part III, § 48), "a family of activities for a family of purposes" (*RFM,* Part V, § 15).

One may want to admit that mathematics may well be a game, a game played according to fixed—compelling—rules and regulations. But one will want to insist that we do not calculate arbitrarily, first this way then that, but rather infer just those conclusions that inexorably follow from our premises. But what do such inferences amount to?

> What we call a "logical inference" is a transformation of our expression. E.g., the translation of one measure into another. Inches are on one edge of a ruler, centimeters on the other. I measure the table in inches and then convert to centimeters *on the ruler.*—And certainly there is correct and incorrect when converting from one measurement to another. But what reality does "correct" correspond to here? No doubt with a *convention,* or a *custom,* and perhaps with practical needs. (*RFM,* Part I, § 9).

But does it not have to be shown that our inferences are justified by laws of inference that are independent of such conventions, customs, and practical needs? Certainly there are such laws, and in fact we often do employ them—for example, when we write down detailed mathematical proofs or present them on the blackboard. But there are other situations in which we speak of "inferring":

> . . . it is necessary to look and see how we make inferences in the course of using language, what sort of process inferring is in the language game.

> E.g.: a regulation says: "Everyone over 1.8 meters tall is to be taken into the . . . department." A clerk [A] reads out the names of the people and their heights. Another [B] separates them into departments.—[A:] "N. N. 1.90 meters." [B:] "So N. N. goes into the . . . department." That is inference. (*RFM*, Part I, § 17).

Should the clerk proceed in any other manner, that would have unfortunate results: he would come into conflict with the law and there could be all sorts of undesired practical consequences. (See *RFM*, Part I, § 116.) But, of course, that does not mean that the laws of society together with practically relevant facts determine the laws of inference and their validity. Rather, it means that what we call "inferring," "thinking," "deducing," etc., exists only under certain circumstances. Many things come together: customs, institutions, the limits of our intellectual powers, facts of the most general sort. These things also contribute to the "motley" of mathematics. And it is decisive that what we *call* "inferring" is a process in which *we* proceed strictly and inexorably. If the process were not strict and inexorable, it would not be inferring; we would not call it inferring:

> Now we talk about the "inexorability" of logic, imagining the laws of logic to be even more inexorable than the laws of nature. We now call attention to the fact that the word "inexorable" is used in several ways. Very general facts of daily experience correspond to our logical laws—facts allowing us to demonstrate those laws again and again in a simple way (e.g., with pen and paper); they can be compared with the facts that make it easy and useful to measure with a meter stick. Very general facts suggest the use of exactly these laws of inference, and now *we* are inexorable in applying them. Because we *"measure";* and it is basic to measuring that everybody uses the same scale. But in addition, one can distinguish inexorable from ambiguous rules of inference—in other words, *unambiguous* rules of inference from those that leave an alternative open to us. (*RFM*, Part I, § 118).

Just how unambiguous and inexorable our mathematical procedures are depends on how we go about using and teaching them. If we draw crooked lines at irregular intervals on a sheet of paper, we quickly loose count of them; if we draw clearly organized and separated groups of lines,

we see at a glance how many there are and can count on a similar immediate and unhesitating response from others. If we combine such figures with additional "gestalts," we can undertake coordinated procedures while achieving with a certain consistency the same results. A change will occur at a certain point in this game, however, namely, when we remove some of the arbitrariness from the process, declaring the regular process to constitute a proof and an especially reliable configuration to constitute the picture of the proof. From now on the game is so played that this configuration is *treated* as an example or model. When comparing two figures, we orient ourselves by means of this clear gestalt—use *this* figure as the measure, *that* as the thing measured. It is not as if we could find out something else by means of our coordinations:

> The proof does not *examine* the essence of the two figures; it expresses what I will take to be part of the essence from now on.—Whatever pertains to the essence, I deposit among the paradigms of language.
>
> The mathematician creates *essence*. (*RFM*, Part I, § 32).

Through our actions—through types of procedures recognized as practical and declared to be such—we establish paradigms, thereby constructing what is essential, so that what belongs to, and corresponds to, the essence is just that way and *cannot* be otherwise. What is essential— counted as essential—does not reside in things themselves, for ". . . 'essential' is the mark of a concept, never the property of an object" (*RFM*, Part I, § 73). When reflecting on the structures of mathematics, which are intangible and at the same time very rigid and inexorable, we lose sight of the fact that we are dealing with a projection of our own decisions and their consequences. We see the sys-

tem of laws lying before us as a newly discovered conti-
nent, whose essence is hidden but now to be explored:[64]

> . . . talking about *essence*—is merely noting a convention.
> But to this one wants to retort: nothing is as far from a
> proposition about the depths of the essence as a proposition
> about a mere convention. But what if I reply: the *depths* of
> the essence correspond to the *deep* need for the convention.
> (*RFM,* Part I, § 74).

In his reflections on mathematics, more than in most
of the other writings, Wittgenstein is concerned with the
exposure of idols. He is especially concerned in these writings, to show (in ever new examples) the delusiveness of
the search for *a single* principle of things, and the delusiveness of the demand for universally valid or absolutely
necessary philosophical knowledge. And he wants to demonstrate that attentively observing the conditions that
actually bring about these erroneous thoughts and endeav-
ors can lead to real—perhaps beneficent, useful, or satisfy-
ing—insights. With these insights, the mathematician no
longer appears to us as someone unable to escape from the
"hardness of the logical must." We come to see him as one
who is:

> . . . always inventing new forms of representation. Some
> inspired by practical, others by aesthetic requirements,—
> and yet others in a variety of ways. Imagine here a landscape
> artist designing paths for a garden; it may well be that he
> sketches them on the drawing board like ornamental ribbon
> and does not even imagine anyone will walk on them.
>
> The mathematician is an inventor, not a discoverer. (*RFM,*
> Part I, § 167f.).

---

64. Cf. *CV,* p. 1 (1929): "In no religious denomination has the misuse of
metaphysical expressions been responsible for so much sin as it has in
mathematics."

4

✳✳✳

Language Games

Investigations

The *Philosophical Investigations* is Wittgenstein's major post-*Tractatus* work. Although he kept refining the manuscript until near the end of his life, it can be said with *some* justification that the book was a completed work when first published in England, two years after his death. The decision of the editors to include the so-called second part was questionable, however, for there is nothing to indicate that this would have been in keeping with the author's intention. Therefore, in the following discussion it is usually "Part I" that is meant whenever referring to the *Investigations*.

There is no decisive answer to the question as to when Wittgenstein began to write the *Philosophical Investigations (PI)*. As noted earlier, there is a sense in which everything he wrote after his return to philosophy was to be part of the planned masterwork. The *PI* does not, however, cover everything he aimed to cover—it has no logico-mathematical part, for instance. It is therefore perhaps more appropriate to say that the work had its beginning in the fall of 1936. Wittgenstein was then in Norway trying to rewrite the book he had dictated in Cambridge, known as the *Brown Book*. (The result is printed in the German edition under the title *Eine philosophische Betrachtung.*) Eventually he came to the conclusion that (as he puts it in a notebook) "this whole attempt at a reworking is *worth nothing.*" He took a new approach and, after months of concentrated effort, produced the early version of the first third of the *PI*. In the following year he composed an additional manuscript, one that corresponds in part to the *Remarks on the Foundations of Mathematics*, Part I. Wittgenstein had these two manuscripts copied, presumably after thorough revisions. Thus the first version of his projected later work consisted of two parts of roughly equal length: the first comprised sections 1–188, approximately, of today's *PI;* the second, Part I of *Remarks on the Foundations of Mathematics.*

In the ensuing period, Wittgenstein was mainly preoccupied with questions in the philosophy of mathematics and did not return to the typed manuscript of the *PI* until the '40s, when he expanded and revised it. Intermediate versions were produced before the last typed manuscript was completed, around 1945/46. (Up to about 1949 or 1950, Wittgenstein made changes even in this manuscript.) We do not know when (if ever) he consciously gave up plans for an accompanying part on the philosophy of mathematics. In any case, from 1944 on he concerned himself hardly at all with mathematical-logical questions. Themes in the philosophy of psychology are what preoccupied him in the second half of the '40s.

By and large, the *PI* is a (for the most part) carefully crafted work. Most of the remarks are short—though not as short as the propositions of the *Tractatus*. But these remarks obviously belong to larger trains of thought, into which—with effort and thought—they can be integrated.[65] Several attempts to structure and organize these trains of thought have been published,[66] but probably everyone who reads the book will prefer his or her own arrangement.

---

65. Wittgenstein said to Drury in 1949: "Every sentence in the *Tractatus* should be seen as the heading of a chapter, needing further exposition. My present style is quite different; I am trying to avoid that error." Drury, "Conversations With Wittgenstein," p. 173.

66. See especially the volumes of commentary by Baker and Hacker (with their very detailed divisions illustrated by diagrams), as well as von Savigny, "Seelische Sachverhalte sind von der sozialen Einbettung abhängig."

A stylistic (but not merely stylistic) peculiarity of the *PI* should be mentioned immediately. Many of the remarks are in the form of dialogues. Because quotation marks sometimes are used, sometimes omitted, some cautions are in order: first, it is not always the same dialogue partner with whom Wittgenstein is arguing; second, the positions taken by the dialogue partners are anything but stupid. Many commentators have made the mistake of failing to take the statements of the dialogue partner seriously, or of dismissing them as caricatures of a philosophical position; they have thereby failed to do justice to either the style or the content of Wittgenstein's writings, since often the dialogue partner's contribution is weighty and meant to be pondered.

One occasionally hears German speakers complain that Wittgenstein uses the informal *du* when addressing the reader. This is not only silly but also incorrect. For the person addressed is Wittgenstein himself, in one of his many roles. Always functioning as his *alter ego*, the dialogue partner voices at different times views of the *Tractatus,* of writings from the '30s, and of a variety of *possible* positions. This is still another reason for taking the dialogue partner's standpoint seriously.

Wittgenstein's understanding of the essence of a philosophical problem is of fundamental importance in assessing the *PI*. "A philosophical problem has the form 'I'm not familiar with the terrain' " (*PI,* § 123): this is not a casual remark but the characterization of an entirely distinctive conception. For whoever is unfamiliar with the terrain will not try to remedy the situation by constructing theories, coming up with speculations, defining new concepts, or contriving minute distinctions; rather, he will attempt to organize his thoughts and gain an overview—for which purpose he may build a model or draw a new map. Whoever is unfamiliar with the terrain will not criticize his surroundings, imagining how much more beautiful they would be if one did this or that, and attempting to reshape them; rather, he will try to get to know and understand them just as they are. He will, above all, want to figure out at the start how he could have lost his way. Having done that, he can at least return to the starting point.

Those who do philosophy often are led astray by language. This happens most of all when we assume that language always functions in the same way: nouns this way, verbs that way, etc.[67] This assumption comes from a bias, a bias quickly revealed as such by attention to the actual use of language in everyday situations. This does not mean, of course, that only everyday uses are legitimate; what it means is that common situations are *more reliable* and that we feel *more secure* in them than in totally unfamiliar situations. If one has often used a screwdriver to take out and put in screws, one will easily manage to use it in analogous situations. But if you want, or need, to use it in an unfamiliar situation (e.g., to open a can), you will be well-advised to think over the possibilities revealed by its past use, and then to carefully apply it as far as possible to the task at hand.

Philosophers—and not *only* philosophers—have often attempted to use familiar expression such as "space," "time," "thing," "property," "think," etc., in ways having little or nothing in common with everyday usage. (Those who *honestly* require examples are referred to any history of philosophy.) In such cases the philosopher may well have a certain meaning in mind, but this meaning may remain in the realm of intention, never having been settled at all. In such cases the philosopher acts like Lewis Carroll's Humpty Dumpty: as if he could fill words with sense and life through a simple act of consciousness. Through a long series of examples, Wittgenstein demonstrates just how easily one can confuse subjective intention with actually available linguistic meaning—that is, with meaning learned and proven in use. A proven means of getting the exuberant metaphysician to see that the meaning he intends is not accessible to others is to describe the everyday use and set

---

67. Cf. ms. no. 213: "The primitive forms of our language—noun, adjective, and verb—show the simple picture to which it tries to make everything conform" (quoted in Kenny, "Wittgenstein on the Nature of Philosophy," p. 49).

it over against the unproven use. It is therefore one of the philosopher's jobs "to return words from their metaphysical to their everyday use" (*PI*, § 116).

If you are not familiar with a terrain, you will try to reach a familiar point from which to orient yourself, rather than conducting your search in the dark unknown. You will then, step by step, and with an eye on the familiar point, investigate new areas, determining whether you can make any progress there with the means at hand. It is therefore quite in keeping with his concept of the problem that Wittgenstein compares language with an old city, with its "maze of alleys and plazas, old and new houses, and houses with additions from various periods" (*PI*, § 18). And he regards his own role as comparable to that of a guide through a city or an unknown country. He describes his task that way in the following passage from lecture notes, characterizing himself (not untypically) as a "bad guide":

> I am trying to conduct you on tours in a certain country. I will try to show that the philosophical difficulties arise . . . because we find ourselves in a strange town and do not know our way. So we must learn the topography by going from one place in the town to another, and from there to another, and so on. And one must do this so often that one knows one's way, either immediately or pretty soon after looking around a bit, wherever one may be set down.
>
> This is an extremely good simile. In order to be a good guide, one should show people the main streets first. But I am an extremely bad guide, and am apt to be led astray by little places of interest, and to dash down side streets before I have shown you the main streets.
>
> The difficulty of philosophy is to find one's way about. The real difficulty in philosophy is a matter of memory— memory of a peculiar sort.—A good guide will take one down each road a hundred times. And just as a guide will show one new streets every day, so I will show you new words. (*LFM*, p. 44).

Although the image of the tour guide is in fact an appropriate characterization of Wittgenstein's method of proceeding, it is rather contemplative in comparison with his best known characterization of the philosophical task: "What is your goal in philosophy?—To show the fly the way out of the fly trap" (*PI*, § 309). The fly in the trap does not behave like the traveler in the strange city: having landed on the sticky surface, it is in grave danger. Lack of orientation is not the only problem: the fly suffers confusion in every part of its being, and is unable to escape from what has seized it. Being rescued from this sort of predicament would be to be rescued from the greatest distress. Of course, one would have to take the problems as seriously as Wittgenstein did in order to be taken captive by them in this way—and then one's rescuer could only be a Wittgenstein.

Games

To the surprise of readers opening it up for the first time, the *Philosophical Investigations* begins with concise descriptions of situations involving the use of words. For all their concreteness and simplicity, these descriptions have the effect of gradually imposing significant philosophical demands. The first description concerns the purchase of five red apples. The second describes two people using language at a construction site:

> We shall imagine a language that fits Augustine's description [of language quoted in § 1]. Let this language serve the purpose of communication between a builder A and his assistant B. A is constructing a building out of building stones: blocks, columns, slabs, and beams. B is to bring the building stones, in the order A needs them. For that purpose they use a language consisting of the words "block," "column," "slab," "beam." A calls out the words and B brings the stone he has learned to bring at this call.— Think of this as a complete, primitive language. (*PI*, § 2).

Although he claims to want to describe a—complete— language, it is striking that what he actually does is to characterize circumstances of use for linguistic expressions.

This emphasis on action and circumstances is typical of Wittgenstein's mature writings. But it is the way language, activity, and circumstances of expression are joined in those writings that makes them interesting, distinctive, and fruitful.

Wittgenstein calls "a complete primitive language," such as the one described in section 2, a *language game.* He had already used this term in the early '30s. At different times and in different connections, various aspects of the language-game concept are in the foreground.

In one respect, the concept of language games simply serves to emphasize the importance of taking context into account when trying to understand or explain the meaning of linguistic expressions. This is not, of course, an original point. And already in the *Tractatus* Wittgenstein had written—in a formulation reminiscent of Frege—that "a name has meaning only in the context of a proposition" (3.3). Wittgenstein recognizes that knowledge of the proposition is not always sufficient for judging the meaning of an expression when he develops the idea of the "*system* of propositions" in his discussions with Waismann (*WVC,* pp. 64ff., 89ff.), and in his *Philosophical Remarks* (p. 59). In the early '30s, Wittgenstein emphasizes, ever more strongly, the parallel concepts of "grammar," "rule," and "calculus."

The idea of language as a calculus underscores the importance of the context that makes it possible for an expression to have a certain function. But Wittgenstein soon found that the word "calculus" conjures up a whole series of unwanted associations. Although "*we* in our discussions constantly compare language with a calculus proceeding according to exact rules," this is "a very one-sided way of looking at language":

> In practice we very rarely use language as such a calculus. For not only do we not think of the rules of usage—of definitions, etc.—while using language, but when we are asked to give such rules, in most cases we aren't able to do so. We are unable clearly to circumscribe the concepts we use; not because we don't know their real definition, but because there is no real "definition" to them. To suppose

> that there *must* be would be like supposing that whenever children play with a ball they play a game according to strict rules. (*BB,* p. 25).

The calculus concept is ill-suited to language because it makes us think of explicitly known usage rules and intimates to us that the expressions we use must be free of vagueness, clearly defined, and exact.

Wittgenstein drops the comparison of language with a calculus or series of calculi in order to avoid these confusions. But "language game" is not simply a less misleading replacement for "calculus"; it also calls attention to factors hardly treated earlier, at least in a connected way. Two of these factors—*nonlinguistic* surroundings and *learning*—are implied in the passage just quoted. But, in the writings of the '30s and '40s, Wittgenstein frequently places the accent elsewhere by bringing out ever-new aspects of the language-game concept. Not just a more appropriate concept for elucidating linguistic meaning, "language game" is closely connected with Wittgenstein's mature conception of the whole task and accomplishment of philosophy. Moreover, clarity is brought to other areas (for example, philosophy of psychology and mathematics) through the description of language games involving particular terms.

One of the earliest formulation of the language-game concept is found in the *Blue Book,* where Wittgenstein speaks of language games as

> ... ways of using signs simpler than those in which we use the signs of our highly complicated everyday language. Language games are the forms of language with which a child begins to make use of words. The study of language games is the study of primitive forms of language or primitive languages. (*BB,* p. 17).

These "primitive" language forms are not, however, basically different from the complex and complicated types of usage of everyday or specialized linguistic expressions. Our ways of acting and reacting are more clearly revealed in the less complicated situation and are less likely to lead us astray. "We see," correspondingly, "that we can build up the more complicated forms from the primitive ones by gradually adding new forms" (*BB*, p. 17). Describing the use of a problematic expression is, in this way, made possible, or easier. And, as Wittgenstein sees it, a successful description is often the best explanation.

It is the *Brown Book* that makes the fullest use of the method of describing language games. Dictated in English in 1934/35 and partially reworked in German in 1936, this text consists essentially of the description of a numbered series of language games, together with concluding commentaries. Language games are here called "systems of communication":

> They are more or less akin to what in ordinary language we call games. Children are taught their native language by means of such games, and here they even have the entertaining character of games. We are not, however, regarding the language games which we describe as incomplete parts of a language, but as languages complete in themselves, as complete systems of human communication. To keep this point of view in mind, it very often is useful to imagine such a simple language to be the entire system of communication of a tribe in a primitive state of society. . . .
>
> (The picture we have of the language of the grown-up is that of a nebulous mass of language, his mother tongue, surrounded by discrete and more or less clear-cut language games, the technical languages.) (*BB*, p. 81; cf. *WLA*, pp. 11–12, pp. 46ff.).

All of these characteristics are mentioned again in subsequent writings, especially in the *Investigations,* and the language-game concept is unquestionably among the central concepts of the later writings. Wittgenstein never developed a *theory* of the language game, however, and any attempt to reconstruct one from scattered remarks would violate his principle that theories have no place in philosophy. (One has a right, of course, to dispute this principle. But an *interpretation* should conform to what is being interpreted so as not to falsify it.) In what follows, the language-game concept will be better illuminated in its various contexts, and elucidated by discussion of relevant questions and objections.

Forms of Life

Why does Wittgenstein use the peculiar concept of "language game"? Isn't playing for children, or for adults without serious work to do at the moment? And isn't the use of language often an important matter—something on the serious rather than the light side of life? Why, then, of all things, speak of "language *games*"?

A part of the answer lies in the formulation of the question itself. Wittgenstein wants to stress that we have to learn linguistic expressions and wants to remind us of how we learn them in the first place. We are not to think of the way adults learn a foreign or technical language, but of the way children learn their mother tongue. Here the "teaching of language is not an explaining but a training" (*PI, § 5*).

Some interpreters are disturbed by the word "training," imagining that it implies approval of a cynical method of education. This worry is completely groundless, however, for Wittgenstein is using the word "training" to express a fundamental philosophical insight, not to advocate a pedagogical method. Wittgenstein wants to make it clear that learners who are to master the rudiments of an activity have no choice but to practice a sort of drill until they learn the required techniques. If they find the activity completely unfamiliar, they will not be in a position even to ask relevant questions. In the beginning, there will be training: on the one side, showing through word and deed; on the other side, imitating and repeating. Whoever wants to learn to play a musical instrument has to be shown where the fingers belong, how one stands or sits, etc. The nature of the training is in this case quite clear. Wittgenstein wants us to see analogous features in the learning of language. The training situation provides the "hard rock" that "bends back my spade" (*PI, § 217*); this is why it is philosophically so important. The training situation provides "hard rock" in two respects. First, the kind of use learned in training cannot be questioned; in the context of training there is no sensible "why?" We learn the color words, for example, in a certain way (the Russians or Eskimos, somewhat differently); taking the original learning processes into account when seeking to understand the concept of color may be relevant precisely because it precludes questions such as "Why is that color called 'red'?" (There is no law against such questions, but they lead us nowhere.)

Second, learning in the training situation is tied to our inborn capacities. Examples make this plain: We do not learn to play the violin with our toes, our fingers being much better suited to the purpose. At first we learn only a few primary colors; we would be unable to cope with a much larger repertoire. What concepts we learn, and in what manner and order, is quite obviously connected with our "human nature." Therefore, we are justified, in view of the learning situation, to speak of this or that as the "natural" use of a certain concept. And we are not using the word "natural" to appeal to naive prejudices or indemonstrable essences; we are appealing, rather, to what is direct, instinctual, and spontaneous.

In this connection it is often objected that Wittgenstein wants to replace linguistic philosophy with child psychology, or with research into language acquisition. For the way we learn our concepts is a "purely contingent" and "empirical" matter, and we could have learned them in an entirely different way.

To the extent that explanation of the meaning of problematic expressions is often thoughtlessly reduced to a description of the learning process, this objection is not without justification. Wittgenstein is not in the least concerned with matters of empirical investigation, however. The point of his remarks on this topic is that the learning of fundamental concepts in training situations is just as "contingent" as the language itself. We can certainly imagine ourselves, or other creatures, learning color concepts in a different way. But, in order to imagine that, we must *tell a coherent story,* that is, describe an imaginary language game. Whether or not the concepts learned in this fictitious situation would be the same as those we actually learn is something that would emerge only in a sufficiently detailed description of the imaginary language game. From comparing the real with the fictitious language game, we can learn something about our actual use of concepts.

Although an "innate concept" is not logically impossible, not all logical possibilities are of philosophical interest. It remains a fact that all of *our* concepts must be learned somehow. Those who assert that the concept of color is always the same, regardless of how it is learned or whether it is learned at all, are guilty of petitio principii. And that color concepts are *not* always the same is confirmed by descriptions of real as well as fictitious language games.

Behind these ideas from Wittgenstein's later period is a conception that he developed quite gradually, out of materials he had uncovered and refined in the '30s. This conception includes: first, the rejection of a thesis that was important both in the *Tractatus* and the earliest writings of the '30s: the thesis that the logic of language can be presented with crystalline clarity (cf. *PI*, §§ 97, 107f.); second, the conviction that understanding language requires insight into the activities in which it is involved. Although the idea that language is always an activity also was espoused by J. L. Austin and other speech-act theorists, Wittgenstein takes it much further when he contends that nonlinguistic factors are necessary for understanding the linguistic.

If for profitably describing the actual use of language it is necessary to take nonlinguistic circumstances into account, then that is also—or all the more—necessary for characterizing a fictional use of language. In a word: "To imagine a language means to imagine a form of life" (*PI*, § 19).

It is clear from his examples that by "a form of life" Wittgenstein means the entirety of the practices of a linguistic community. But it was not his purpose to summarize the activities of an epoch or that of a particular group or society. The main focus of his interest was the connec-

tion between linguistic expressions and habitual actions—
that is, actions hardly noticed because they seem so natural. Nor does this imply that Wittgenstein excluded new
types of linguistic construction, merely that these constructions would have to play a different—perhaps more fleeting
and difficult—role than do the everyday expressions of our
language. A form of life, like a language, may be compared
to an old city, with its "maze of alleys and plazas, old and
new houses, and houses with additions from various periods; all this surrounded by a number of new suburbs with
straight, regular streets and uniform houses" (*PI*, § 18).

What seems strange or familiar to us depends on our
form of life. But the existence of common instinctive reactions in primitive training situations makes it possible for
us to understand even the strange and unfamiliar. We can
extrapolate from primitive, banal situations, succeeding,
thereby, to "see a face" even in an unfamiliar form of action. Although we cannot read the expression of the face as
directly as we read the expression of a face in surroundings familiar to us, we still can attempt to interpret it. We
can, in a similar way, come to understand an unknown
language: for "common human behavior is the system of
reference by means of which we interpret a foreign tongue"
(*PI*, § 206).

The emphasis is always on the practical side of human
expressions: "The term 'language *game*' is meant to emphasize that the speaking of a language is part of an activity or a form of life" (*PI*, § 23). Everything that strikes us
as natural goes to shape our form of life and our language
as well; the hypothetical, the merely intended, is rather
meaningless in this connection. "People agree in *language;*
this is agreement in form of life rather than opinions" (*PI*,
§ 241). Wittgenstein's point is not that our experiences and
views about the world play no role. His point is that there
is not just *one* group of factors that make linguistic communication possible. Thus:

> Communication by means of language requires not only
> agreement in definitions, but also (strange as it may sound)
> agreement in judgments. This seems to put an end to logic,

but it does not.—It is one thing to describe methods of measuring, and another thing to get and express the results of measuring. But what we call "measuring" is also determined by a certain constancy in the results of measuring. (*PI*, § 242).

The distinction between the "judgments" in the preceding quotation and the "opinions" in the passage before that is not a matter of syntactical form. It depends on the way certain propositions function in our lives. Through their functions, these propositions become parts of the framework of language (and its "logic"). The *Investigations* contain no clearer formulation of this matter; it is not until his final period, in remarks from *On Certainty,* that Wittgenstein attempts to more clearly delineate the distinct functions alluded to here.

Family Resemblances

Wittgenstein used the phrase "language games" to bring out the role of training and natural capacities in learning language and to emphasize that language is an activity; he also used it in connection with the problem of comparing and identifying various types of linguistic activity. One can see that there is a problem here by the fact that Wittgenstein designated extremely various types of language use as "language games." Thus, on the one hand he speaks of language games characterized by the use of certain individual words, and on the other hand he speaks of the use of language per se as "the language game":

> We can also imagine that the whole procedure of the use of words in (2)[68] is one of those games through which children learn their mother tongue. I want to call these games *"language games"* and sometimes speak of a primitive language as a language game.

---

68. That is, the language game described in section 2 of *Philosophical Investigations* and quoted in this chapter on p. 102.

And one could call the processes of naming the stones and repeating words after someone language games too. Think of some of the uses made of words in round dances.

The whole, the language and the activities with which it is interwoven: this I will also call the "language game." (*PI*, § 7).

The kinds of language games named here are not easily brought under a common denominator. And it is Wittgenstein's conviction that it would be unproductive to follow the usual philosophical practice of seeking the characteristics common to everything that might be called a "language game." According to Wittgenstein, this striving to formulate the "essence" of a thing—that is, common characteristics deemed to be necessary and sufficient for its existence—has led us astray again and again. Also misleading is the uniform and homogeneous appearance of the written word, which disguises the fact that words cannot all be understood according to some one schema, such as "All words signify something" or "There are two basic types of words, those that signify something and those that don't." Wittgenstein uses an analogy to bring out the variety of words: "Think of the tools in a tool chest. There is a hammer, pliers, a saw, a screwdriver, a ruler, a glue jar, glue, nails, and screws.—The function of words is as varied as the functions of these objects. (And in both cases there are similarities.)" (*PI*, § 11).

Wittgenstein does not, of course, want to deny the existence of concepts whose proper use depends on the presence of common characteristics—concepts found most of all in the formal and empirical sciences. But he wants to stress the existence of the many concepts in everyday language whose correct use depends on the presence not of common characteristics but of incomplete similarities.

Wittgenstein uses the word "game" to bring out the type of similarity he has in mind:

Consider, for example, the proceedings we call "games." I mean board games, card games, ball games, athletic games, etc. What is common to all of these?—Don't say: "They *have to* have something in common or they would not be called 'games' "—but rather *look and see* if there is something common to all of them.—For if you do look at them, you will not see something common to *all;* you will see similarities and relationships—a whole series of them. As I said: don't think, look!—Look, for example at the board games with their variety of related features. Now go on to the card games: here you will find many things that correspond to the first group, but many common traits disappear while others appear for the first time. If we move on to ball games, much that is common is retained, but much is lost. . . . And we can proceed through the many, many other groups of games in the same way, seeing similarities surface and disappear.

And the result of this investigation is like this: We see a complicated network of similarities intersecting and overlapping one another—similarities large and small. I can give no better characterization of these similarities than "family resemblances"; for it is in just this way that the various resemblances to be found among members of a family overlap and intersect: build, facial features, eye color, gait, temperament, etc., etc.—And I will say: 'games' form a family. (*PI,* §§ 66f.).

This conception of family resemblances marks one of the decisive points where Wittgenstein breaks with the philosophical tradition. He reveals how inadequate the traditional "same concept, same characteristics" model is, especially in the area of everyday expressions with very comprehensive ranges of application—which is the area from which philosophy draws its central concepts ("space," "time," "soul," "thinking," "freedom," etc.). Wittgenstein does not, however, attack the traditional position out of an invincible skepticism or an excessive impulse for destruction. He wants to prove that the tradition errs because it too crudely strives for generality[69] and because it feeds on

---

69. "This craving for generality is the resultant of a number of tendencies connected with particular philosophical confusions. There is—

(a) the tendency to look for something in common to all the entities which we commonly subsume under a general term.—We are inclined to think

a "one-sided diet" of examples.[70] On the other hand, he offers in the idea of family resemblances an elaboration of the conception shaken by his critique, an elaboration that, if accepted, completely removes from the old conception what made it so attractive—the element of unambiguous decisiveness for all possible cases.

"Game" is thus Wittgenstein's preferred example of a concept that applies to things that do not all possess a common characteristic but do all show some family resemblances. This, no doubt, was not the least of Wittgenstein's reasons for forming the compound "language game," for with this phrase he suggests that, like other types of games, language games can have family resemblances without sharing an essential characteristic. His intention becomes clear when he permits his conversation partner to raise the following objection:

> You make it easy for yourself! You speak of all kinds of language games but nowhere say what is essential to a language game and so to language. What is common to all these proceedings that makes them language, or parts of language?

To this Wittgenstein replies:

---

that there must be something in common to all games, say, and that this common property is the justification for applying the general term 'game' to the various games; whereas games form a *family*, the members of which have family likenesses. Some of them have the same nose, others have the same eyebrows and others again the same way of walking; and these likenesses overlap. The idea of a general concept being a common property of its particular instances connects up with other primitive, too-simple, ideas of the structure of language. It is comparable to the idea that *properties* are *ingredients* of the things which have the properties; e.g. that beauty is an ingredient of all beautiful things as alcohol is of beer and wine, and that we therefore could have pure beauty, unadulterated by anything that is beautiful.

(b) . . . ." (*BB,* p. 17).

70. "A main cause of philosophical sicknesses—a one-sided diet: one nourishes one's thinking with only one kind of example" (§ 593).

> Instead of producing something common to everything we
> call language, I say that no one thing is common to all these
> phenomena that makes us use the same word for each,—
> but that they are *related* to one another in many different
> ways. And it is because of this relationship or these
> relationships that we call them all "languages." (*PI*, § 65).

While not, therefore, altogether uniform activities, language games are nevertheless related among themselves. As with other games, rules are of determining significance for many sorts of language games. Some are quite circumscribed by rules; others, in which rules and regularity are just hinted at, are borderline cases of rule-governed activities. Partly by pointing out explicit rules of the language game, partly by referring to other conventions, it can be shown what a *move* in the language game amounts to. This concept is especially important with regard to Wittgenstein's more general thoughts in philosophy of language. The naming of things, he says, "is no move in the language game." Just as setting up the chess figures is not a move in the game of chess, but rather serves (at most) as a preparation for later moves, so the naming of things is not as such part of the course of the game. This consideration places our use of names and other terms in a new, unaccustomed light. Whether or not an action is to be regarded as a move in the language game depends on the *point* we ascribe to it, or to a certain way of playing it. The point of a game can be its purpose, its utility, or our joy in playing it. The point of a game is mentioned in order to indicate *why* it is played, *why* one makes a certain move. Here a more or less specific explanation should be given. What you state as the point of the game or move may be something extremely general ("to win") or something quite specific ("to lull my opponent into a false sense of security"), depending on your audience and the aspect of the game you want to explain. The game's point depends on its being embedded in a suitable environment. If certain normal conditions are not fulfilled, if anarchy prevails, then the game loses its point. Thus: "The procedure of putting pieces of cheese on the scale and determining the price by the reading would lose its point if it became common for such pieces suddenly to shrink or grow for no apparent reason" (*PI*, § 142).

Rules

Games often are played according to more or less explicitly established rules. But *rules*, like *games*, form a "family," with no precisely delineated defining characteristic. Already in the *Blue Book* (pp. 12f.) Wittgenstein had called attention to the fact that rules fulfill very different purposes depending on whether one says that relevant activities are *in accordance* with the rules or that they *involve* the rules. Rules for the use of "red" and cardinal numbers are explicitly involved in the shopping activity described in the first paragraph of the *Philosophical Investigations*. Although normal shopping certainly would not be described as involving such a use of rules, one could say that it is "in accord with" such and such rules. But in that case one could always formulate new rules with which the activity might justifiably be said to accord.

The multiplicity of relations between rule and game is a theme of the *Investigations*. Thus, in answering the question "What is the rule by which he proceeds?" Wittgenstein lists the following possibilities: "The hypothesis that satisfactorily describes his use of words, which we observe; or the rule that he looks up when using the signs; or what he gives us as the answer when we ask him about his rule" (*PI*, § 82). The way we answer the question about the rule will depend on the way the question was asked. But an answer is not always possible, for "is there not the case where we play and—make up the rules as we go along? . . . [and the case where we] modify them—as we go along?" (*PI*, § 83).

Not every aspect of a game is determined by rules. For example, tennis is a game though no rule exists for how high or hard the ball may be hit (*PI*, § 68). Although there is always the theoretical possibility of doubting whether a certain action corresponds to the rule, usually no one actually doubts. And the existence of a normal case—where action is unimpugned by doubt—is not merely an empirical observation; rather, it points to a state of affairs important for the very *concept* of game. By "game" we do not mean "an activity whose rules preclude all doubt and stop up all the holes" (*PI*, § 84), but an activity only partially determined by rules.

Reflection on the relationship between games and rules becomes philosophically acute as soon as one takes language games into consideration. On the one hand, it can be revealing to compare the use of linguistic expressions with behavior in the framework of a carefully regulated game: certain linguistic "moves" simply become clearer to us when we juxtapose them with the exactly established possibilities of a calculus-like game. On the other hand, time and time again our actual use of language deviates from the ideal. But we must be careful here. We are easily led astray by this talk of the ideal:

> If one now says that our language *only approaches* such calculi, one is standing on the edge of a misunderstanding. For then it can appear that we were speaking in the logic of an *ideal* language. As if, so to speak, our logic were a logic for a vacuum.—While in fact logic does not treat of language—or thinking—in the sense in which a natural science treats of natural phenomena, and one can at most say that we *construct* ideal languages. But here the word "ideal" would be misleading, for it suggests that these languages would be better, more complete, than our everyday language—as though it took a logician finally to show people what a proposition looked like. (*PI*, § 81).

The difference between operating with language and operating with a calculus is not the presence of greater rigor in the latter. To be sure, the card game skat is in certain ways a more "rigorous" or "strictly determined" game than hide-and-seek or cops and robbers; this is not, however, because it more strictly follows similar sorts of rules. Much more, it is because the rules themselves differ in kind and in the roles they play. Similarly, rules function differently in language than they do in a calculus. The fundamental difference is in the games themselves, not just in our attitude toward possible mistakes or violations of the rules.

The irritating thing about the relationship of rules to their use is that not even the most precise formulation of a rule guarantees its flawless execution. Misunderstanding is always possible because the rule does not compel compliance with itself—in the way consuming salty food causes thirst. As with the ostensive explanation, the rule leaves much open; it cannot force me to make the right application. Many of the open possibilities look absurd to us when pointed out, however; for we learn the application cf the rule when we learn the relevant practice. And when we want to execute the relevant activity, alternative interpretations of the rule do not even occur to us, for we do not connect them with this way of acting.

Wittgenstein compares the rule to a signpost (*PI,* § 85). If you stop to think about it, a signpost does not really determine how one is to proceed. It does not specify whether one must stay on the road or may cut across the fields, nor does it even say in what direction to go, for it doesn't tell me to follow the direction of the point rather than the blunt end—I can interpret it in either way. But something is queer about this line of thought, for I can make use of a signpost if I know what it is and how it functions. I do not have to *interpret* it at all in order to find out how I am to follow it to reach my destination. If its point points to the right and it says "To the summit," while I (who want to go to the summit) turn to the left, this is not a matter of an excusable or allowable (mis)interpretation. It shows that I just do not know what a signpost is or how it functions. Correctly using the sign depends not on my correctly interpreting it, but on my having learned how one follows it— that is, in my having acquired a practical ability.

One learns how to follow the rule by being habituated to certain reactions and procedures so that one can perform them automatically. It might be objected, however, that here we are referring to a simple causal connection, which cannot remove our philosophical doubts. The reference to practical training indicates "that we follow signposts only to the extent that there is a regular use of signposts, or a custom" (*PI*, § 198). But to this it may be objected that the need for a practice and a conventional procedure is a plain, philosophically insignificant fact.

Accordingly, the objector will construct the following "paradox":[71] Inasmuch as the rule—like the signpost—is unable to determine any way of acting, every way of acting can somehow be brought into conformity with it. I can follow the signpost in this, or the opposite, direction; both possibilities are open to me. In just the same way, every way of acting can be interpreted as going against the rule. Since no possibility can be excluded, all talk of agreement or the opposite is senseless.

This "paradox" is the expression of a misunderstanding of the relationship between rule and activity. Every rule certainly can be interpreted in any way. The misunderstanding lies in comparing "acting according to the rule" with *interpreting* the rule. Acting according to the rule is really acting within the framework of a certain practice—a practice in which there is training and supervision, hence also right and wrong. This connection between rule and action is not only factual but also (as Wittgenstein puts it) "grammatical." If acting in accordance with a rule of a game were something like an interpretation of the rule, there would be no need for games as institutions. One could then formulate a new interpretation each time—something that would turn things upside down. For it is only within the framework of a game that rules have their point.

Of course, one can learn a game by reading rules of play (and understanding them correctly), but that is possible only because one already has learned similar games. Interpretation must be anchored in training at some point.

---

71. Kripke in *Wittgenstein on Rules and Private Language* gives a completely different interpretation from that presented here. His view is that Wittgenstein himself uses the paradox to ground a certain skeptical attitude. Baker and Hacker's *Skepticism, Rules and Language* contains an (only partly successful) critique of Kripke.

Thus what winning and losing mean is learned not by studying rules but by watching people at play and their reactions, and by joining in the game with them. This is a practical context that remains unintelligible without practice in these or similar procedures. Another reason for including the practical context in an account of "acting according to rules" is that a bare "interpretation hangs in the air along with what is interpreted" (*PI*, § 198). It becomes possible to doubt and interpret rules and actions only when rules and actions are bound up with our customs and practical procedures. Doubting whether *A* handled the ball according to the rules makes sense only against the background of a normally doubt-free practice. And the possibility of interpreting a rule this or that way in a special situation exists only because everything else does *not* require interpretation.

The concept of following a rule is inseparably connected with the idea of a practical way of acting. It would be a misuse of the word "rule" to say of someone having no practical knowledge of the relevant game that he is following its rules. If he thinks he is following the rules but, for example, is unable to demonstrate standard moves or to correct the wrong moves of others, then we have no right to assume that he is following them. To interpret a rule means simply to replace one formulation of the rule with another.

> Therefore "to follow a rule" is a practice. And to *think* one is following a rule is not the same as following it. And therefore one cannot follow the rule "privately," because otherwise thinking one is following a rule would be the same as following it. (*PI*, § 202).

This conception has consequences for philosophy of language as well as philosophical psychology. In both areas, concepts not anchored in procedures open to examination are declared worthless. As objects of philosophical investigation, the linguistic as well as the psychological require public criteria; we cannot really know what we are talking about without these criteria.

Paradigms

Philosophical understanding, as Wittgenstein sees it, does not result from setting up theories of the highest generality. In fact, it is often the striving for generality that leads us astray. Painstakingly collecting all imaginable individual details and setting up specific theories based on them is not, however, any better than the unbridled striving for generality. This could not help us reach the insights we hope to gain through philosophy; it would be just a further attempt to imitate the sciences. The task of philosophy is not one of clarifying the unknown and mysterious; it is that of placing in a new light things that we constantly have before us but are no longer aware of, so that we can perceive them and correct the false images that have led our thoughts astray.

> Philosophy merely puts everything before us; it explains and infers nothing.—Since everything is plainly there, there is nothing to explain. For what is concealed does not interest us.
>
> One could also call "philosophy" what is possible *before* all new discoveries and inventions. (*PI*, § 126).

The "inventions" alluded to are technical inventions based on scientific knowledge. Other "inventions" do pertain to the philosophical enterprise: invented stories about foreign tribes, unknown societies, and fantastic educational systems. Through *comparison* with representations of actual relationships or invented situations, such stories can help us to a better understanding of the possible applications of our concepts. The comparison with invented language-game situations—the "fictitious language games" spoken of previously—puts our actual concepts through a stress test, as it were, showing how far their application extends and where they reach their limits.

If one clearly keeps the thrust of this procedure in view, it is evident that a view often attributed to Wittgenstein is misplaced. This view—that new or different circumstances automatically call forth new or different concepts—actually is repudiated by Wittgenstein: "I am not saying (in the sense of an hypothesis) that if this or that fact of nature were different, then people would have different concepts" (p. 230). Whether or not concepts would have to adapt to the new circumstances by changing is not immediately foreseeable and is without philosophical interest. The philosophical task is to understand *our* concepts better and to present them more clearly, and for this we need simple, pregnant, intelligible examples that permit a comparison. Invented illustrations often serve this purpose much better than actual examples, for with them we can emphasize *the* aspects that permit a comparison to have a particularly revealing effect. "Our clear and simple language games are not preliminary studies for a future regularization of language—in the nature of first approximations, ignoring friction and wind resistance. Rather, the language games are set up as *objects of comparison* meant to throw light on circumstances of our language through similarities and dissimilarities." (*PI*, § 130).

The work of the philosopher is like that of the painter who wants to reproduce a certain view of the circumstances as exactly as possible. Such a painter cannot simply "reproduce" nature point by point, color by color, shape by shape. He must constantly simplify and build in elements that do not even exist in order to create a convincing picture of reality. In a similar way, the philosopher also must frequently introduce simplifications and fictitious elements into his presentation, so as to make overview and comparison possible.[72]

There are various ways of comparing states of affairs or objects with one another. One can place things side by side and see how they relate to one another. In this case it is most important to provide an overview, to group the

---

72. In a note written in 1947, Wittgenstein compared his own work with that of an impressionistic painter whose intentions are constantly being thwarted by the traditional way of seeing and painting: "It is as if I *wanted* to paint an impressionistic picture but were still so caught up in the old manner of painting and therefore, in spite of every effort, kept on painting what one does *not* see. For example, I strive for far more detail than is needed or desirable." Cited in Schulte, *Erlebnis und Ausdruck*, p. 34.

things to be compared in a certain way, and to divide them so that one recognizes at a glance what the relationships are. ("Don't think, look!") Another method of comparison is to measure against a certain pattern. Here the things are arranged by checking how they relate to a very specific object. This object has a special place in the checking procedure: it is not measured; it is the measure. If one places a piece of cloth next to a meter stick, it is usually clear that what is measured is the length of the cloth, not the length of the meter stick. Not knowing this would not be like holding two handkerchiefs side by side and being unable to decide which to choose. If you do not know what a measure is and what a thing measured, then you must first be taught the whole practice of measuring the length of things. Once you have learned that, the question as to what is to measure against what no longer exists.

The activity of measuring and the special place of the measuring device is a recurrent theme in Wittgenstein's philosophy. In the *Tractatus* we read: "The picture is connected *thus* with reality; it reaches out to it. It is like a ruler applied to reality. Only the most extreme points of the graduation marks actually *touch* the measured object" (2.1511–2.15121). In conversations with Waismann and Schlick the new concept of a system of propositions is introduced through the idea of a measure: "A *system of propositions* is like a ruler applied to reality. By this I mean the following. If I apply a ruler to an object in space, then I apply *all the graduation marks* at the same time" (*WVC*, p. 63f; cf. illustrations on pp. 64 and 76). In philosophy of mathematics the idea of measuring and of the ruler's special role also comes up again and again. For example: "The proof is our model of a certain *yield*, which serves as an object of comparison (ruler) for real transformations. . . . Even if the proven mathematical proposition seems to point to a reality beyond itself, it is only the expression of the recognition of a new measure (of reality)" (*RFM*, Part III, § 24, 27).

"Measurement" and the special role of the measuring rod are treated again in the *Philosophical Investigations,*

in connection with an extremely suggestive—and disputed—
example:

> There is *one* thing about which one cannot say either that
> it is or is not one meter long, and that is the standard meter
> in Paris.—This is not, of course, to ascribe some sort of
> strange characteristic to the latter; it is merely to
> characterize its special role in the game of measuring with
> the meter stick.—Let us imagine samples of color preserved
> in Paris like the standard meter. We define "sepia" as the
> color of the hermetically sealed standard sepia kept there.
> Then it will make no sense to say of this sample that has
> this color, or that it hasn't. (*PI,* § 50).

Many misunderstandings of this passage have resulted from
trying to explain it independently of Wittgenstein's conception of language games. It then appears that Wittgenstein
was denying that there are *any circumstances* in which
one could say that the standard meter is of such and such
a length.[73] And that is exactly what Wittgenstein did not
say; rather, he pointed out that an object having, in the
(language) game of measuring, the very special role of measure or final check, cannot in *this* game be sensibly regarded as an object to be measured. That does not mean
however that it cannot be measured under any circumstances; it means, simply, that one changes language game
A if what serves as measure becomes the thing measured.
The standard meter in *A* can, of course, become the thing
measured in game *B;* in game *B* it is meaningful, and
perhaps true, to say "the standard meter is not a meter
long."

A second sort of misunderstanding involves the use of
the word "sense." The objection has been raised against
Wittgenstein that even if the sentence "The standard meter
is not one meter long" is always false, it still always makes
sense. It makes sense because it is syntactically correct,

---

73. Kripke has also misunderstood this passage. See *Naming and Necessity,*
pp. 54f.

contains no undefined words, and clearly presents the conditions under which it is true or false. Here a concept of sense is applied to Wittgenstein's thoughts with which Wittgenstein himself did not agree—a concept that he defended himself against to some extent. Of course, even he would agree that, in many cases, the stated conditions are minimum conditions of sense. But he would insist that additional conditions often must be considered when determining linguistic sense. In the first place, the expression (sentence) in question must (as I said above) be a *move* in the relevant language game; second, it must have a *point* in this language game. In the language game or games in which the standard meter has the role of the primary standard, saying "The standard meter is not a meter long" is not a permissible move, and has no point. It is *for this reason* that Wittgenstein concludes that it has no sense, and so it is a misunderstanding (at best) if one disputes his statement on the basis of a completely different concept of sense.

Building on the "standard meter" example, Wittgenstein develops his more extensive conception of the *sample* or *paradigm* in the same section:

> This sample [the standard sepia] is an instrument of language by means of which we make statements about color. In this game it functions not as something represented but as a means of representation. . . . What apparently *has to be the case* is part of language. It is a paradigm in our game—something with which comparisons are made. And, although this may be an important point, it remains a point about our language game—our method of representation.

Here Wittgenstein simultaneously and precisely formulates several basic ideas. What functions as a sample, object of comparison, or paradigm in the language game is on the same level as the words used in it. This means not that the standard meter and color sample thereby change into words or other linguistic units, but that they—like the words— are indispensable means of description and understanding in the language game. Consider the example of a color atlas with its numerous color samples. These samples are in a certain sense nothing more than paper printed in colors. If, however, it is a question of naming and judging the colors of pictures reproduced in another book, the atlas plays a very special role. When placed next to the reproductions, these samples are measures, not objects measured; they function as the standards we need to make our comparisons.

It is tempting to make all sorts of statements about *necessary* relationships if we contemplate these samples independently of their role in the language game. For instance: "Between these two colors there *must* be an additional shade" and "This color *must* be brighter than that one," etc. But these are not necessities inherent in the matter; rather, the appearance of necessity is a consequence of how in the game we project on reality the grid produced by the paradigms we use. When we use "must" in such propositions we are talking not about the reality observed but about our system of representing it. The appearance of necessity is due to a confusion of levels: we think we are talking about relationships between things but are really talking about the language games in which certain things are given a special role—a role they do not have in other games, where they are just things among other things. For this reason, the word "apparently" is important in "What apparently *must* be is part of language."[74] The erroneous impression of necessity stems from overlooking the relationship of the thing in question to the linguistic level.

Use

It is only against the background of the language-game conception that the following famous dictum becomes intelligible:

---

74. In the *Tractatus* Wittgenstein says that there is no necessity except that of logic (6.375). Things said in the *Tractatus* with reference to logic are analogous to passages in the later writings that refer to language or grammar.

> For a *large* class of cases of the use of the word "meaning"—
> even if not for *all* cases—the word can be explained thus:
> The meaning of a word is its use in language. (*PI*, § 43).

What to understand by "use" here is clear only when taking into account what Wittgenstein means by "point" and "move" in connection with a language game. One has to understand that the variety of linguistic uses cannot be forced into the same mold, but are related to each other by "family resemblances." And it is important to recognize that certain linguistic and nonlinguistic items (expressions, samples, paradigms) fulfill a very special function in which they must be understood as measures rather than as things measured. And we have seen that the application of language cannot be correctly interpreted until one sees how it engages with our form of life—how it (like various kinds of tools) fulfills diverse tasks in various ways. Language is most intimately connected with form of life; a given concept describes a "pattern in the weave of life recurring in different variations" (*PI*, p. 174).

The thesis of meaning as use is opposed to the sort of conception found in the passage from Augustine quoted at the beginning of the *Investigations*. This conception conveys

> ... a certain picture of the essence of human language: that the words of language name objects—that propositions are combinations of such names.—In this picture of language we find the roots of the following idea: Every word has a meaning. This meaning is correlated with the word. It is the object for which the word stands. (*PI*, § 1).

This picture determines a whole series of ideas that are subsequently taken to task—for example: Russell's idea that the demonstrative pronoun "this" is the only genuine name; the *Tractatus'* naming theory of meaning.

Wittgenstein insists on distinguishing the meaning of a name[75] from its bearer—"the *meaning* of a name is sometimes explained by pointing to its *bearer*" (*PI*, § 43). The

---

75. Strawson raised the objection that one can speak of the meaning of a *name* only in quite special circumstances—when, for example, one says

idea presented by Frege and taken over in the *Tractatus,*
that the meaning of a name is the object to which it refers,
is therefore misleading, because the meaning can live long
after the bearer has ceased to exist. Simple as it seems,
this insight is of major importance in that it enables us to
criticize the numerous representatives of the philosophical
tradition, from Plato to the author of the *Tractatus,* who
accepted the necessity of positing indestructible primary
elements in one form or another.

Here as elsewhere, the tenor of Wittgenstein's remarks
is that no *simple* concept will really help. It will lead us
astray by inviting generalizations that falsify the use of
the concept. For example, suppose I were asked whether
Moses really existed. I would reply that he certainly existed to the extent that most of the characteristics attributed to him in the Bible pertain to one and the same person, and to the extent that the actions ascribed to him
there were carried out by just this person. Should it turn
out that one of these characteristics does not correctly apply, I still hold fast to my conviction, for "Haven't I got
ready a whole series of props, so to speak, so that I can
lean on one if another is taken away, and vice versa?" (*PI,*
§ 79). Certainly, if more and more statements about Moses
are shown to be untrue, I will at some point have to admit
that Moses did not exist. But there is no *determinate* point,
given by a rule or some other determination, at which the
old judgment has to be revoked; the idea of such a point is,
indeed, incompatible with the conception of linguistic use

---

that "Peter" means "stone"; "Giovanni" means "John"; etc. This objection
takes the normal use of language as sacrosanct—an attitude quite foreign
to Wittgenstein. For of all the novelty of his thought, he thinks and
expresses himself here within the framework of a philosophical tradition
that leaves room for the conceptions of the meaning of a proper name—for
the conception he represents as well as the one he criticizes. As long as no
errors arise out of it, it makes absolutely no difference to Wittgenstein
whether or not his use of language is in harmony with that of an idealized
"normal speaker": "Say what you want, as long as it does not stop you from
seeing the facts. (And when you see them, there is much that you will not
say.)" (*PI,* § 79). See Strawson's 1954 review of the *Investigations,* reprinted
in Strawson, *Freedom and Resentment.*

developed by Wittgenstein: "I use the name 'N' without a *fixed* meaning. (But that is no more detrimental to its use than it is detrimental to the use of a table that it's four-legged instead of three, and may therefore wobble in certain circumstances") (*PI*, § 79).

5

***

Criteria

Verification and Criteria

Wittgenstein's writings in the first years after his return to philosophy emphasize a number of concepts that are tied to radical views. Subsequently elaborated in an ever more complex manner, these concepts become more fully interrelated and eventually lose much of their radical character. Finally—at about the time of the first draft of the *Investigations*—they coalesce into a unity. The concepts in question are "verification," "calculus," "rule," "grammar," and a few others. Losing something of their centrality and becoming more limited and specific, all of these concepts meet in an organic conception that can perhaps best be characterized by the wider concept of "language game." Although largely inadequate compared with later, often extremely complex, thoughts, the earlier ideas have the merit of highlighting certain features that otherwise would have been easily overlooked.

The idea characteristic of the first period after the return to Cambridge—that the sense of a proposition is its verification[76]—is gradually qualified and modified. This means neither that Wittgenstein dismisses the importance of verification nor that he gives up the principle of verification, namely the idea (considered as objectionable then as now) that there is an intimate connection between linguistic meaning and (real or possible) procedures of verification. Wittgenstein never took seriously the objection that

---

76. Cf. *WVC*, p. 47 (12/22/29).

he was mixing up questions of meaning and questions of verification—that is, mixing up theory of meaning and theory of knowledge. For first, he had no patience with such *theories,* and second, he counted breaking down the walls separating these supposedly disparate areas among the goals of his philosophy.

In a 1932–33 lecture Wittgenstein alludes to a criticism that accused him of mixing up problems and procedures belonging to different areas:

> Some people say that the question, "How can one know such a thing?," is irrelevant to the question, "What is the meaning?" But an answer gives the meaning by showing the relation of the proposition to other propositions. That is, it shows what it follows from and what follows from it. It gives the grammar of the proposition, which is what the question, "What would it be like for it to be true?," asks for. In physics, for example, we ask for the meaning of a statement in terms of its verification. (*WLA,* pp. 19–20).

He says in another passage, by way of elucidation, that the verification of a proposition serves to determine the meaning of the expressions contained in it insofar as it has to do with grammar, while it does not serve to determine meaning in so far as it is a matter of experience (see *WLA,* p. 31).

A description of the verification procedure is not, to be sure, a definition or any other direct statement of meaning. But it illuminates an important aspect of the application—the "grammar"—of linguistic expressions, thereby helping to determine their meaning. In a revealing passage from the 1932–33 lecture notes, Wittgenstein jumps suddenly from "different ways of verifying" to "criteria," remarking:

> We can distinguish between primary and secondary criteria of its raining. If someone asks, "What is rain?," you can point to rain falling, or pour some water from a watering can. These constitute primary criteria. Wet pavements constitute a secondary criterion and determine the meaning of "rain" in a less important way. (*WLA,* p. 28).

While not answering all questions, the distinction thus indicated does anticipate the more detailed differentiation in the following well-known passage from the *Blue Book:*

> Let us introduce two antithetical terms in order to avoid certain elementary confusions: To the question "How do you know that so-and-so is the case?," we sometimes answer by giving 'criteria' and sometimes by giving 'symptoms.' If medical science calls angina an inflammation caused by a particular bacillus, and we ask in a particular case "why do you say this man has got angina?" then the answer "I have found the bacillus so-and-so in his blood" gives us the criterion, or what we may call the defining criterion of angina. If on the other hand the answer was, "His throat is inflamed," this might give us a symptom of angina. I call "symptom" a phenomenon of which experience has taught us that it coincided, in some way or other, with the phenomenon which is our defining criterion. (*BB,* pp. 24–25).

Wittgenstein briefly returns to this distinction in the *Philosophical Investigations:* "The fluctuation in grammar between criteria and symptoms makes it seem as though there are only symptoms" (§ 354). He thought that one reason this incorrect impression arises is that we imagine that whatever is in any way dependent on experience is subject to the possibility of sensory illusion—so that what we took to be a defining criterion turns out to be only a symptom. What this overlooks, according to Wittgenstein, is that whatever is simulated in an illusion remains, through the meaning of the relevant expressions, connected to certain criteria (and "definitions"). I can assume from my friend's sullen facial expression that he is in a bad mood, and be wrong. But that the sullen expression seems to me to reflect my friend's *mood* (rather than the status of his bank account or the situation in Poland) is connected with the *concepts* "sullen," "facial expression," "mood," etc.; it is not just a matter of experience.

Wittgenstein frequently stresses that the connection here is closer than that between past experience and present impression. The conditions Wittgenstein takes as criteria are not in every case sufficient or necessary to prove the applicability of the relevant concept, as several interpreters have correctly observed. But their further claim that Wittgenstein postulates a special "criterial" relation between some concepts and certain conditions of their application is without adequate support, as far I can see. The ways of behaving Wittgenstein calls criteria for the presence of mental states, or the correct use of psychological expressions, certainly do not provide an infallible basis for attributing the appropriate predicates. We nevertheless, in many cases, will see a conceptual—"grammatical" or "logical"—connection between such criteria and that to which they point. The postulation of a sui generis "criterial relation," however, does nothing to illuminate the examples described by Wittgenstein.

Here are some examples of criteria: the report of a dream is a criterion for the fact that someone dreamed this and that; *X*'s confessing that he had such and such a thought is a criterion for correctly guessing what *X* was thinking; certain behaviors are criteria for someone's being in pain, being happy, being able to multiply, etc. As a criterion for whether someone is *reading,* one checks whether he can answer certain questions, attends to his expression, checks whether he reacts the same way to other texts, etc. In this connection it is important that *one* criterion is not alone decisive for all cases, but that "we also use the word 'read' for a family of cases." "And we apply different criteria in different circumstances for someone's reading" (*PI,* § 164).

Criteria play a role in two main areas for Wittgenstein. The first concerns criteria of identity, which supposedly permit answers to questions such as whether we are dealing with one object or several. The second area concerns the attribution of states of consciousness, feelings, etc.; it is here, above all, that the asymmetries between "first" and "third person" emerge.

Persons

In a rather early manuscript, in a passage dealing with the objects designated by proper names, Wittgenstein expressed a conception of the identity criterion still frequently used in analytic philosophy:

> If we give spatial objects names, then our application of these names is based on a criterion of identity that presupposes the continuity of movement of bodies and their impenetrability. So if I were able to do with two bodies A and B what I am able to do with their shadows on the wall—make one out of the two, two out of one—then the question of which of the two bodies is A and which is B after the separation is senseless. I could go on to introduce a completely new criterion of identity, e.g., the path of their movements. (For the name of a river created from the confluence of two rivers there is such rule: . . . The resulting river receives the name of the source-river in whose approximate direction it flows onward.) (*PG*, p. 203).

If it is questionable whether an object a at time t_1 is the same as an object b at time t_2, we attempt to determine whether a track that is continuous in space and time can be reconstructed between a and b. If no such reconstruction is possible, then the question remains open; if it is revealed that the track of a leads in a different direction from that of b—if there is, therefore, a demonstrable discontinuity—we conclude that a and b are not identical. Spatio-temporal continuity is our main criterion for the identity of material objects.

The problems get more complicated if one asks about personal identity, as Locke did in a well-known passage of the *Essay*.[77] For in dealing with questions about whether a is the same person as b, we usually not only use the criteria associated with material objects but also take into consideration such things as whether someone suffering from amnesia or a radical change of character is the same person as before. In normal cases, we apply all three criteria—spatio-temporal continuity, consistency of memory, and continuity of character—and practically always find all three of them fulfilled; therefore, our concept of a person is put under extreme stress if a discrepancy appears when these criteria are applied. A resolution is not provided for,

---

77. Book II, Chap. 27.

and because the concept of personal identity is so important because of its many moral and social implications, we are unhappy to have to fix its use through an arbitrary decision.

We can perhaps clarify the limits of the concept if we consciously put it to the test by inventing situations in which—as if with a distortion mirror—the conditions of its application are altered so as to as to see how far the usual criteria help. With consummate skill, and obvious pleasure in the invention of ludicrous situations, Wittgenstein puts concepts under pressure by freely varying the conditions of their application. This procedure is in keeping with the maxim: "Whoever thinks that certain concepts are absolutely the correct ones, so that anyone who has different ones would be failing to see something that we see,—let him imagine certain very common facts of nature to be different from what we are used to, and other concept-formations will become intelligible to him" (*PI,* Part II, § xii; cf. *RPP,* Vol. I, § 643).

Where Wittgenstein had earlier spoken of logical multiplicity, in the early 1930s he occasionally used the word "geometry" to indicate the extent and scope of a concept. With the help of fictitious situations, he wanted to show how different the "geometries" bound up with our concepts are, once placed in modified surroundings. Suppose the circumstances of the application of "person" changed radically. What "geometry" of the concept of person would then strike us as natural?

> Imagine, e.g., that all human bodies which exist looked alike, that on the other hand, different sets of characteristics seemed, as it were, to change their habitation among these bodies. Such a set of characteristics might be, say, mildness, together with a high pitched voice, and slow movements, or a choleric temperament, a deep voice, and jerky movements, and such like. Under such circumstances, although it would be possible to give the bodies names, we should perhaps be as little inclined to do so as we are to give names to the chairs of our dining-room set. On the other hand, it might be useful to give names to the sets of characteristics, and the use of these names would now *roughly* correspond

to the personal names in our present language. (*BB,* pp. 61–62).

So in such a situation, continuity of character would be the decisive criterion of personal identity. We would, accordingly, use personal [proper] names. But suppose we lived in a world in which all human organisms alternatively manifested two different sets of characteristics—a world in which it was *normal* for people to act like both Dr. Jekyll and Mr. Hyde; it would then be appropriate to speak of double personality and to give each of the two distinct personalities its own name. Wittgenstein spins out a further possibility: a world in which people express different memories on odd- and even-numbered calendar days. Here we would no doubt be inclined to group continuous memories together and to regard the presence of such groupings as the determining criterion of personal identity. This decision certainly would not be compelling, for ". . . I am at liberty to choose between many uses, that is, between many different kinds of analogy. One might say in such a case that the term 'personality' hasn't got one legitimate heir only" (*BB,* p. 62). What changes with the shifting of the weight of the various criteria is the use of the concept, and, consequently, its meaning. Such a change in meaning can be uncomfortable; thus, where possible, we prefer to retain the old criteria despite changed conditions, desiring to stay with the "geometry" to which we are accustomed.

Pain

Criteria of personal identity are used when, for example, we want to determine who performed a certain action or who can give us certain information. In connection with this point, Wittgenstein describes a case that at first makes a strange impression:

> What does it mean to know *who* it is who is in pain? It means, for example, to know which person in this room is in pain—the one sitting over there, the one standing in the corner, the tall blond person over there, etc.—What am I

driving at? That there are very different criteria for personal *'identity.'*

So which is it that determines my saying that *'I'* am in pain? None at all. (*PI,* § 404).

This brief answer sums up an entire series of reflections on the various "first" and "third person" asymmetries that had occupied Wittgenstein throughout the '30s and for a large part of the '40s.[78]

Again and again he returns to the point that the utterances through which I make known my own pain function differently from utterances about your pain or the pain of a third party. There are several reasons for the choice of pain as an example, the most important one being that no one thinks of pain as subject to the will. By discussing pain, one avoids the problems that would arise in discussing feelings, where one can speak in terms of degrees of voluntariness. A second reason for Wittgenstein's consistent focus on pain is the internal connection between pain and its expression. In the expression of other feelings or sensations, linguistic and nonlinguistic conventions play an important role, thus obstructing our view of the natural/instinctive connection between a feeling and its expression. The expression is, however, usually quite direct in the case of pains; we do not give thought to whether and how we are to express our pains.

Wittgenstein began to explore the first/third-person asymmetries shortly after his return to philosophy. Most of all in the context of his argument with solipsism, it struck him how complicated the use of the pronoun "I" is, and how easily the philosopher can be tricked by it. In *Philosophical Remarks* Wittgenstein employs a series of thought-experiments to gain clarity. For example:

> The concept of the toothache as feeling-datum is, to be sure, as applicable to the tooth of another as it is to mine, but only

---

78. We are using "first person" as short for "first person singular," and "third person" to cover all the remaining grammatical "persons." Statements involving "he" or "they" will in this context be the standard examples, rather than expressions involving "you" or "we."

in the sense that it might be perfectly possible to feel pain in a tooth that is in somebody else's mouth. According to our present way of speaking, one would not express this in the words "I feel his toothache," but rather in the words "I have pain in his tooth."—One can say: Of course you do not have his toothache, for it is now very well possible that he will say, "I do not feel anything in this tooth." Am I to reply, "You're lying, I feel how your tooth aches"? (*PR*, p. 92).

All of these reflections lead to one conclusion: "With pains I distinguish intensity, location, etc., but no owner" (*PR*, p. 94). In other words: When pains are *felt*, criteria of personal identity do not come into play; one simply *has* pains, one does not ask "Am I really the one who has these pains?" Verification and the application of criteria come into play only when it is a question of the sensations or feelings of other persons. I do not myself need to *attribute* my sensations to myself; I at most *express* them.

Thinking that both pronouns can be replaced by proper names, one all too quickly places the use of "he" and "I" on the same logical plane. But this placement is completely wrong. The word "I" is not used like a name and can only rarely be replaced by one without distorting the meaning of the original sentence. In order to be able to appreciate Wittgenstein's remarks on "asymmetry" and the peculiarities in the use of the pronoun "I," however, we must first be clear about the nature and weight of the philosophical errors that can result from not acknowledging his insights.

Errors

If we place the use of "I" on the same plane as the other personal pronouns, we are led to misconstrue both uses and thereby are led into far-reaching philosophical errors. A typical case of ascribing a feeling would be one in which we observe the behavior of a friend and, on the basis of that, form the judgment, "He's not feeling well; he's depressed." As to what this judgment means, two sorts of things will be put forward by way of explanation. On the one hand, we will describe "how things appear to him inwardly," saying, for example, that he sees everything in

shades of grey, that he looks on the dark side of everything, that he constantly thinks of unpleasant events and
everything makes him sad. On the other hand, we will
refer to consequences, predicting that he would only morosely shake his head if asked to dance, that he would not
laugh if told a funny story, that he would speak of the
fruitlessness of all earthly endeavor if we tried to incite
him to action. These are things we would cite in order to
explain the concepts "not feeling well" and "depressed," as
well as for the characterization of the anticipated behavior.
Whether this explanation is understood depends on many
factors that are now of no relevance. Whether or not the
prediction is true depends on whether our friend really
behaves in the manner predicted. And of course we can be
mistaken in all this: our friend may not really be depressed
even though he seems so to us; if he is depressed, he may
not act in the way we predict, in spite of his depression.

   These and other imponderables associated with this
use of concepts for states of consciousness, perceptions,
and feelings can hardly be eliminated. But everything seems
suddenly to change if I start to speak about myself. If I say
that I don't feel well and am depressed, I can explain what
I mean by saying that I see everything in shades of grey,
etc., and that if asked to dance I would morosely decline,
and so forth (much as in the earlier explanation). Here we
do not have to reckon with the possibility of erroneous
information; rather, when I say I feel miserable, that settles
it.

   Comparing first and third person statements with each
other produces the impression that while everything I say
about the other person is chancy, everything I say about
myself is absolutely certain and irrefutable. It is correct
that a falsification of my judgment cannot be precluded
when I am talking about the other person. If, on the other
hand, I say of myself that I do not feel well and am depressed or in pain or homesick, then (assuming no underlying self-deception at work) I cannot be mistaken—but
also I cannot be right. I can be right only where I also can
be making a mistake. When I say "I'm tired," I can be lying
but I cannot be making a mistake. It is clearly nonsense to

talk of confusing one feeling with another or of being mistaken as to what person I am talking about here. Error,
doubt, conjecture, and guessing are precluded in one's own
case; it is therefore senseless to speak of absolute certainty
here either. The possibility of contrast gives the use of the
word its sense.

There is another way to characterize the error we are
inclined to make in considering these problems: We think
of statements about the psychological state of another person by analogy with statements about the contents of his
pockets. We know from experience that he carries this and
that around with him; we see him take out cigarettes and
assume that he also has matches. These are things about
which we can believe and conjecture—and *know* something.
If I see him put his handkerchief in his pocket, I know he
has a handkerchief there. If I know that he has carried his
keys in his pocket for fifty years, I am certain that they are
there today too. It is no different when it comes to the
contents of my own pants pockets. I can believe that this
or that is in my pocket, can be sure that I have my keys,
can know that the handkerchief is in my pocket. But I can
be just as wrong about the contents of my pocket as the
next person.

Looking at states of consciousness and perceptions from
this point of view, it appears as if I can make no mistakes
about my own mind's "pocket," while I can always do so
where the mind of another is concerned. But here the point
is not that I am more certain in my own case, have better
knowledge, know my way around, or the like. When I say
that I am homesick, I am not basing that on some kind of
evidence; rather, I am *exhibiting* my feeling. When I say
that I am in pain, this is not a proposition that rests on
absolutely certain conclusions drawn from indubitable evidence; it is the direct expression of my sensation—I am
exhibiting pain, not knowledge.

The statement that the other person is depressed can
be incorrect because I can be in error regarding his feelings and regarding his identity. Because there are no criteria involved at all, the utterance that I am depressed can,
in an important sense, be neither correct nor incorrect. I

can lie about it, or say something I didn't mean to say, but I cannot be mistaken. And the "can" here is the "can" of logical possibility and impossibility.

The contents of my pants pockets or of your pants pockets can always be illuminated by showing them and by using clarifying gestures. I say that I have a package of chewing tobacco in my pocket and the other person asks me what that is. I pull it out, say "It's chewing tobacco," explain what one does with it using the analogy of chewing gum, etc. But if I am talking about my homesickness, this possibility is denied me, even if I feel it very intensely and am tempted to lay my hand on my heart and say I feel it there. Homesickness is neither linguistically nor in any other way "a something" that can in any manner be shown or demonstrated, even though language gives us the strong illusion that it is. Wittgenstein describes a case of this kind in the following passage from *Philosophical Investigations:*

> I have seen someone in a discussion of this subject strike his chest and say: "But no one else can have THIS pain!"—The reply is that one does not define a criterion of identity by the emphatic stressing of the word "this." What this emphasis does is to wrongly suggest the case where we are familiar with such a criterion but need to be reminded of it. (§ 253)[79]

Privacy

Comparing sensations to objects in a box is typical of the philosophical way of looking at things in which one

79. Indeed, the gesture itself can be revealing. In *Remarks on the Philosophy of Psychology* Wittgenstein mentions a whole series of psychologically interesting possibilities for making the observation of gestures (especially instinctive/involuntary gestures) philosophically useful. The following is a frequently quoted example: " 'In my heart I have determined on it.' And one is even inclined to point to one's breast as one says it. Psychologically this way of speaking should be taken seriously. Why should it be taken less seriously that the assertion that belief is a state of mind? (Luther: 'Faith is under the left nipple.')." *PI,* § 589.

focuses on a picture associated with the concept being considered. As obvious and natural as it may seem, such a picture can at times falsify the use of our expressions—especially when it leads us to oversimplify the complicated conditions and circumstances of the actual use of language, and to set up or endorse misleading theories.

It seems correct that we can always be mistaken about the sensations of another person; this leads to the idea of "a something" directly accessible only to the other person—a something about which he is never mistaken but about which we can only guess. That not all is right with this idea is something we already have shown. But again and again, and from different angles, Wittgenstein pursues philosophically significant consequences of the idea that sensations are directly accessible to only to the one who has them, while others can only infer or guess them—the idea summed up in the words, "Sensations are private."

These words express a platitude. While not, of course, incorrect, it can be very misleading, like other platitudes. It has a function, as a "grammatical proposition," either to explain the use of an expression to the uninformed, or to remind someone who has misused the word of its correct application. Imagine that my friend says to me with exaggerated certainty, "I see you're down in the dumps. Come on, I'll buy you a drink." I am not feeling that way at all (but rather, for example, preoccupied or angry) and point out that he does not know what is going on in me at all. "Leave me alone," I say, "you have no idea what I'm feeling. Feelings are private." No fault, whether linguistic or philosophical, is to be found with this response. Although it certainly has no philosophical pretensions, it has its function in the language game, as a rebuff or correction. It is not a substantive statement about the nature of feelings, rather it remains entirely in the realm of grammar. Thus, as Wittgenstein says in the *Philosophical Investigations:* "The proposition 'Sensations are private' is comparable to 'Solitaire is played alone' " (§ 248). That solitaire is played by oneself is not an informative statement about a card game; it is more like a correction to someone who is either ignorant of, or misusing, the concept "solitaire."

One can imagine the following objection to this line of thought: That may be true for *our* language, but ours is only one of many actual and possible languages; imagining a language in which "Sensations are private" has real content and states something about the nature of feelings would surely be helpful in the exploration of conceptual possibilities. Wittgenstein investigates whether a language would be thinkable "in which one could write down or speak out his own inner experiences—sensations, moods, etc.— for his own use"

> —But can't we do that in our own ordinary language?—But I do not mean it that way. The words of this language are to refer to what only the speaker can know—to his immediate private sensations. Therefore, someone else cannot understand this language. (*PI*, § 243).

The language intended here is supposed to be "necessarily," not contingently, private: it is impossible for it to be "spoken" by more than one person. Many of Wittgenstein's reflections are directed, explicitly or indirectly, against the notion that such a private language is possible.[80] Connected with these reflections is the refutation of the idea of "following a rule privately." This refutation is based on the idea that one cannot meaningfully say that only one single person followed a rule only one single time. One cannot meaningfully say this because a rule has to be part of a practice that is institutionalized in some way or other; thus, the rule of a game exists only as something belonging to a game; a law must have a judicial and social framework, etc. An allegedly private following of a rule would amount to nothing more than an imagined following of a

---

80. It is occasionally objected that Wittgenstein's remarks on "private language" are irrelevant because hardly any philosopher had advocated such a conception. This objection misses the mark inasmuch as all representatives of Cartesian dualism have relied on a conception related to this idea, as have the great majority of classical empiricists. Moreover, the notion of a "language of thought," a notion supported by numerous cognitive psychologists and other "artificial intelligence" enthusiasts, is in effect a naive parody of the position Wittgenstein attacked.

rule. All the customary consequences of rule-following are lacking, and the person involved can, at most, believe that he is acting in accordance with the rule. But "*to believe* one is following a rule is not: to follow it. Therefore, one cannot follow a rule 'privatim,' for otherwise to believe one is following a rule would be the same as to follow it" (*PI*, § 202).[81]

Further grounds for rejecting the possibility of a private language can be reached by combining linguistic-philosophical insights from other contexts with the following attempt to construct such a private language:

> Let us imagine this case. I want to keep a diary on the recurrence of a certain sensation. For this purpose, I associate it with the sign "S" and write this sign in a calendar for each day I have the sensation.—I want first of all to remark that a definition of the sign cannot be expressed.—Still, I can give it to myself as a kind of ostensive definition!—How so? Can I point to the sensation?—Not in the usual sense. But I speak or write the sign while concentrating my attention on the sensation—and so, as it were, point to it inwardly.— But why this ceremony? For that is all it appears to be! A definition must serve to fix the meaning of a sign.—Well, that happens by my concentrating my attention, thereby impressing on myself the connection between the sign and the sensation.—"I impress it upon myself" can only mean that this procedure has the effect of *correctly* reminding me of the connection in the future. But here, of course, I have no criterion of correctness. One would like to say: whatever will appear correct to me is correct. And that only means that there can be no talk of 'correct' here. (*PI*, § 258).

---

81. Kripke argued in *Wittgenstein on Rules and Private Language* that the private language problem is actually settled in what is presented and quoted here, and that what comes after § 243 is argumentive and of relatively little significance. He is right that the ideas expressed before 243 are useful when considering the private language argument. But he makes the same mistake as many other interpreters in thinking that there is just one, or just one unique, problem involved here. In reality, the private language problem described in 243 represents a whole complex of additional questions. Subsequent, as well as preceding, sections pertain to the formulation and solution of these questions.

This remark contains two decisive objections to the possibility of a private language. The first relates to the wrongness of the idea of a private, ostensive definition; the second, to the indispensability of criteria for the correctness of a performance. Ostensive definitions play an especially important role in teaching and learning a language. Some words—for example, color words, many words for everyday articles, and even many number words—we learn with the help of ostensive explanations. Ostensive explanation consists in pointing to an object and pronouncing the customary designation, or in demonstrating an action while the expressions to be learned are pronounced with particular stress and accompanied by appropriate gestures. Of course, such explanations guarantee success just as little as do other kinds of explanation. They are unfailingly vague and ambiguous and can therefore always be misunderstood. Thus, their use makes sense only in a context in which misunderstandings can be cleared away. (Of course, the possibility of new misunderstandings cannot be excluded.) In order to clear up and remove misunderstandings in connection with ostensive explanation, the learner must be able to ask questions relating to the type or kind of object in question:

> The ostensive definition explains the use—the meaning—
> of the word, if it is already clear what role the word is
> supposed to play in the language. Thus if I know that
> someone wants to explain a color word to me, then the
> ostensive explanation "That's called 'sepia'" will help me to
> understand the word. . . . One has to know (or be able to do)
> something already in order to be able to ask what something
> is called. (*PI,* § 30).

This means that the learner must have at least mastered the basics of the language game in which the word to be learned plays a role—which is not, of course, to say that he must be able to formulate its rules. It means only that he possesses the practical ability to participate in the game, and (in normal circumstances) to tell whether others are playing it correctly or incorrectly. The existence of this ability depends on the possibility both of correcting the learner and of getting him to ask questions.

Not all of these conditions are fulfilled in the case of the imagined private ostensive definition. Although the ostensive explanation usually does require the presence of a teacher as well as a learner, the decisive thing is not the number of persons present, but the possibility for correction, for questions and answers, and for the removal of misunderstandings—a possibility that would not exist in the "private case." (In fact, this possibility precludes privacy inasmuch as it requires that the game and its essential criteria be of a *public* nature. It is not necessary for there to be a number of persons actually present; the requirement is for publicity in principle.) Talk of a private, ostensive definition—and of that part of the notion of a "necessarily private language" dependent on it—is, therefore, senseless.

The second reason for rejecting the possibility of a necessarily private language depends on the principle that one may speak of "correct" and "incorrect" only where there are criteria that allow us (at least in principle) to check the statements in question. In the case of the first-person *utterance* of pain, I need no criteria—indeed, there are no criteria—but there is also no "correct" or "incorrect" either, inasmuch as such utterances offer no point of attack for possible criticisms. But if it is possible to get something right it also must be possible to get it wrong, and wherever one can be wrong, a public examination must be possible—even if I am myself representing my own "public." But neither criteria nor publicity nor any kind of intersubjective examination and confirmation are possible within the framework of the envisioned private language—and that speaks against calling it "language." For we really want to speak of an expression as part of language only when its use can be justified—which means independently checked.[82]

---

82. Cf. *PI*, § 265: "But justification consists in appealing to something independent.—'But surely I can appeal from one memory to another. I don't know (e.g.) if I have remembered the time of departure of a train correctly, and to check it I call to mind how a page of the time-table looked. Isn't it the same here?'—No; for this process must now really call up the *correct* memory. If the mental image of the time-table could not itself be *examined* for correctness, how could it confirm the correctness of the first memory? (As if someone were to buy several copies of the morning paper to assure himself that what it said was true.)/ Looking up a table in the imagination is no more looking up a table than the image of the result of an imagined experiment is the result of an experiment."

At least *one* reason for the attractiveness of the notion of the possibility of a private language is that the complex of ideas and pictures that appear to give sense to it are rooted in language—or, rather, in a misunderstanding of our language. Wittgenstein uses a simile to elucidate this:

> Suppose that everybody has a box with something in it, which we call a "beetle." No one can ever see into the other's box, and everybody says that he knows what a beetle is only by looking at his own beetle.—It could happen that everyone has a different thing in his box. Indeed, one could imagine that such a thing is constantly changing.—But what if these people's word "beetle" still had a use?—Then the use would not be that of designating a thing. The thing in the box would not belong to the language game at all, not even as a *something:* for the box could be empty.—No, we can "factor out" this thing in the box; it cancels itself out, whatever it is.
>
> That is to say: if one construes the grammar of the expression of sensation according to the model of "object and designation," then the object drops out of consideration as irrelevant. (*PI*, § 293).

The decisive statements here are: first, that the grammar of the expression of sensation may not be interpreted according to the model of "object and designation"; and second, that (insofar as they have a use) words for sensations, states of consciousness, etc. ("beetle"), are not used to designate objects.[83] Borrowed from a primitive use of language, the idea that all words are to be interpreted according to the "name/designated object" model readily misleads us into thinking that all expressions must stand for something named by them. When pain is mentioned, we react to it in terms of this "magical" model, attempting to fix our

---

83. Some interpreters say that if the expression of sensation is not construed according to the model of "object and designation," the object does *not* fall out of consideration as irrelevant. That is a misunderstanding, for if one does not construe this expression in the way criticized, one wouldn't talk at all of an object in the first place; so of course one wouldn't talk of an object remaining either.

attention on what "pain" stands for. We suppose that in some sense mental states and processes resemble familiar states and processes—even though we cannot determine their constitution more closely, or compare and contrast them with others. "The decisive step in the conjurer's trick is taken, and it seemed innocent enough" (*PI*, § 308).

It is not only the misplaced "object and designation" model that misleads us here, however; it is also the fact that we tend to accept a false interpretation of the *use* of our expressions of sensation. Conceptualizing the expression of sensation as the *description* of sensation, we interpret this presumed description as though its exclusive function were to render what is felt. Here there is a compound error: In the first place, expressions of sensation are not only—or perhaps even mainly—used to describe our mental life; in the second place, such descriptions, when actually given, do not necessarily function according to the schema: situation to be rendered/faithful rendering. We tend all too easily to forget that a description usually has a point: it is to serve a purpose or fulfill a task, rather than to just be catalogued like a reproduction made for its own sake.[84]

So much for the critical side of Wittgenstein's reflections. Can these reflections help free us from the dilemma he points out? Do they contain a new conception that will help us to avoid further mistakes? Wittgenstein does not develop—and surely would reject—a new conception in the sense of a theory. The first lesson to be learned from Wittgenstein's "treatment" of the problem is that no simple conception will serve to further understanding. The second lesson is that we are not to allow ourselves to be led astray

---

84. "Perhaps this word 'describe' tricks us here. I say 'I describe my state of mind' and 'I describe my room'. You need to call to mind the differences between the language games. / What we call *'descriptions'* are instruments for particular uses. Think of a machine-drawing, a cross-section, an elevation with measurements, which an engineer has in front of him. There is something misleading about the characterization of a description as a word-picture of the facts: one tends to think only of such pictures as hang on our walls, pictures that seem simply to portray how a thing looks, what it is like—pictures that are idle, as it were" (*PI*, §§ 290f.).

by any alleged model of language. So we are not to construe every expression according to the "object and designation" schema; rather, we are to pay attention to the language game in which we use expressions of sensation and
to what purpose we use these expressions. The confusing
initial question as to the relationship between linguistic
expression and experienced sensation can be reformulated
as follows:

> The question is the same as this one: how does a person
> learn the meaning of the names of sensations—of the word
> "pain," for example? Here is one possibility: Words are
> associated with the primitive, natural expression of the
> sensation and used in its place. A child hurts itself and
> cries; the grown-ups talk to it and teach it exclamations
> and, later, sentences. They teach the child new pain
> behavior.
>
> "So you are saying that the word 'pain' actually means
> crying?"—On the contrary, the verbal expression of pain
> replaces the crying and does not describe it. (*PI*, § 244).

Replacing the question of the connecting or designating
relationship with the question of how particular expressions are learned helps us to see that the connection established between expression and sensation resides in
prelinguistic reactions—reactions upon which an ever more
complex linguistic practice develops. Asking what the new
expression of feeling designates gets us nowhere. Instead
of asking that, we should consider to what extent the expression replaces the prelinguistic behavior and to what
extent it goes beyond that behavior. This way of looking at
things can make it clear that

> . . . a cry, that cannot be called a description, which is more
> primitive than any description, nevertheless serves as the
> description of the inner life.
>
> And it is this service that matters. (*PI*, pp. 189 and 178; cf.
> p. 179).

Emphasizing, as he does, the conceptual connection
between the mental (sensations, states of consciousness,

etc.) and behavior, Wittgenstein has again and again been taken for (or criticized as) a behaviorist. It certainly should be clear that he is not a dualist, Cartesian or otherwise— although some interpreters actually have managed the trick of presenting him as one! He is not to be called a behaviorist either. Not only does he explicitly disavow behaviorism, his position is incompatible with it. In the first place, the way he presents the employment of psychological expressions is far too complex for a behaviorist theory. Second, he at no time attempts to reduce psychological concepts to behavioral concepts. Third, in his descriptions he always avoids opposing the psychological and the physical (mind and body), just as he always avoids reducing the one to the other. Wittgenstein's remarks on philosophy of psychology are consistently so framed that classical and contemporary mind-body problems are precluded. Perhaps some readers are uncomfortable with this because they would like to categorize Wittgenstein's philosophy according to the familiar terminology of dualism and monism, mentalism and behaviorism, etc. But trying to classify Wittgenstein's ideas in such a manner can only distort them.

Aspects

In the second half of the 1940s Wittgenstein was occupied mainly with what he termed "psychological" concepts. Not only were his last lectures at Cambridge on this theme, but his writings from 1945/46 up until his trip to America in 1949 are almost exclusively concerned with aspect perception, sensations, memory, experience, and the like. The handwritten notebooks from this period fill more than eight large ledger books. Approximately half of this material also exists in two typed manuscripts; manuscripts that have been published as *Remarks on the Philosophy of Psychology*. The last manuscript entries, from October 1948 to May 1949, have appeared under the title *Last Writings on the Philosophy of Psychology*. An excerpt of material on philosophy of psychology prepared by Wittgenstein himself was published as "Part II" of the *Philosophical Investigations*.

None of the notebooks in question are organized. In most cases the individual remarks are in the order in which they occurred to Wittgenstein; they do not, therefore, make for easy reading. Although orienting oneself requires constantly consulting the index, working through these materials is worth the effort, because they contain some of Wittgenstein's most fully developed ideas.

In some passages Wittgenstein undertakes a kind of classification of psychological concepts. At one point he divides "concepts of experience" [*Erlebnisbegriffe*] into concepts for experiences [*Erfahrungen*], emotions, and convictions; he then subdivides these. Another time he distinguishes sense impressions, representations, and emotions. Although he is satisfied with none of these classifications, the criteria in terms of which he makes them are interesting. He utilizes the asymmetries between the first and the third person, that is, the contrast between "utterances" and "communications" or "descriptions." He characterizes some sensations as having "real duration," others as involving a characteristic blending, still others as revealing something about the external world. But all of these considerations come to a stop after a few attempts: the whole attempt is too insistent on universal validity—too "theoretical"—for Wittgenstein. A thoroughgoing systematic procedure is not suited to psychological concepts, according to Wittgenstein:

> The concepts of psychology are just everyday concepts. Not concepts newly formed by science for its purposes, like those of physics and chemistry. Psychological concepts are to the concepts of the exact sciences as the remedies of old wives are to the concepts of scientific medicine. (*RPP*, Vol. II, § 62).

Wittgenstein takes a series of examples from William James's *The Principles of Psychology* (1890). But by 1947, at the latest, he draws from a new source, Wolfgang Köhler's introduction to gestalt psychology. He takes illustrations from this and a few other (mainly gestalt-oriented) psychology books, several of which are printed in the *Philo-*

sophical Investigations—for example, the famous duck-rabbit picture that can be seen now as a duck's head, now as a rabbit's.

What is the philosophical interest in figures that can be "seen" in various ways? The question itself suggests a problem, for in a certain sense we "see" the same thing. Although we always see (for example) the same tree in the puzzle picture, until we discover the thief in the foliage, the visual impression (as we call it) has no more changed than the picture itself. Wittgenstein makes the very simple figure of an "F" with its cross lines extended a little to the left the subject of numerous reflections. He asks:

> . . . what does it mean to see the figure first one way then another? Do I really see something different each time, or do I just *interpret* what I see in a different way? I am inclined to go along with the former answer. *But why?* Interpreting is an activity. This interpreting can consist in one's saying "That's supposed to be an F," or in copying it as an F, or in asking oneself "What might it be, an ill-formed 'F'?," etc. Seeing is not an activity, but a state. (A grammatical remark.) And if I never read the figure as anything but an "F," never asked myself what it might be, then one who knows that it can be seen otherwise will say that I see it as an F. (*RPP,* Vol. I, § 1).

From the examination of such examples, and with the help of such "grammatical" points, Wittgenstein draws the important conclusion that introspection is no help in such cases. Delving deeply into the inner picture yields no information about the secrets of the gestalt switch. Wittgenstein therefore changes the direction of the inquiry, examining the various possible situations in which one could say: "So and so does *not* see the aspect" or "is not *in a position* to perceive an aspect change."

One could object that the seeing of aspects and of aspect changes is not among the more significant accomplishments of the human mind. What then is so important about this kind of investigation? Though certainly not as an answer to this objection, Wittgenstein mentions several contexts in which the ability to perceive aspects plays a role—including the context of hearing and interpreting works of music. Directions such as Schumann's "As from a great distance" (*RPP,* Vol. I, § 250) are found in musical scores, and it can happen that an interpreter does not understand them and is not able to play the piece correctly. How can we teach him? (Note the recurrence of the theme of *learning* a skill.) One possibility is to play or sing it for him. Another is to introduce analogies—referring, perhaps, to an Eichendorff poem where a similar feeling is expressed. Or one tells a story, underscoring the pertinent elements through exaggerated gestures or vocal emphases. The decisive thing is that the "aspect" that lies in this "As from a great distance" is tied to a number of characteristic actions, stories, gestures, and analogies, so that, in describing or presenting these, one prepares the way for the emergence of the missing aspect. It is like a jigsaw puzzle: after a certain number of pieces have been put together for him, a beginner finds it easier to complete it by himself. In the case of a practical skill, such as interpreting musical works, it can certainly happen that the student never learns it. One must, nevertheless, hold on to the important insight that the perception of such aspects is connected with, and can be explained with reference to, types of action and gesture, together with certain techniques and procedures of rendering. The aspect is not necessarily hidden, not something that must elude communication.

Other aspects that may escape or elude careful observation are nuances and ambiguities of meaning. Wittgenstein provides illustrations of varying degrees of subtlety. The final "a" in the name "Maria" will be heard differently depending on whether it occurs in "Maria Callas" or in "Rainer Maria Rilke." Another case is the old German joke about Wotan who, instead of giving ground at the command "*Weiche,* Wotan, *weiche!*" ["*Yield,* Wotan, *yield!*"] brings *weichgekochte Eier* [soft-boiled eggs]. Wittgenstein cites a nice example from Grillparzer's journals: "I cannot describe what an eerie impression the *h* in the English word ghost makes on me. When the word is spoken, it doesn't sound particularly special; but if I see it written before me, the effect never fails: I think I am seeing a spirit."[85] Wittgenstein refers to people with no eye or ear for such nuances as "meaning blind" or "aspect blind."[86] What such people lack is a certain sensibility, a certain ability to taste and discriminate:

> But remember how the names of famous poets and composers seem to have absorbed their own meaning so that one can say: the names "Beethoven" and "Mozart" not only sound different; they are accompanied by a different *character*. But if you were to describe this character more closely, would you show the pictures of the composers in question, or play their music?
>
> Back to the meaning-blind person: He would not sense that the—heard or seen—names are distinguished by an imponderable something. And what would he have lost thereby? . . . (*RPP*, Vol. I, § 243).

Aspect-blind and meaning-blind people do exist. They include people who miss certain refinements of poetry, musicians who cannot interpret Schumann, people who never get the point of a play on words. So they miss out on a certain enjoyment that perhaps is not at all important to them. But that is not the point. The meaning experiences and experiences of seeing an aspect are (as already stated) connected in a typical way with certain actions and gestures. Most important, they can be described in a characteristic manner. Those who want to describe the experience of a sudden change of meaning will make use of very specific words, saying, for instance, that one meaning has "changed" into the other, that the "lighting" is different, that the "dull" is now "sharp," etc. It is through such characteristic formulations that we make *what* we feel under-

---

85. Cf. *RPP*, Vol. II, § 572: "Different people are very different in how sensitive they are about changes in the spelling of a word. And the feeling is not just one of piety for an old usage.—If for you spelling is just a practical question, the feeling you lack is like the one a meaning-blind man would lack."

86. Cf. *PI*, Part II, § xi, p. 214.

standable to listeners, for such experiences have typical *expressions* that can be connected with instinctive ways of reacting and with learned skills as well. Appealing to analogies such as "Think of Eichendorff when you play this passage from Schumann" presupposes a lot of ability and experience on the part of the musician. Other expressions of experience are quite immediate. "The vowel *e* is yellow [*Gelb*]" is an example frequently employed by Wittgenstein. According to him, this expression "goes with experience just as the primitive expression of pain goes with pain" (*RPP*, Vol. II, § 574). Analogies, gestures, descriptions, instinctive utterances—these and similar modes of expression help us to understand other people. They are *criteria* for others having certain experiences.

6

✳✳✳

Certainty

Knowledge

A large part of Wittgenstein's writings from the last one and a half years of his life is concerned with the theme of "certainty." Most of this material is contained in *On Certainty,* a book that first appeared in 1969; some of it is in Part III of *Remarks on Color.*[87]

On Certainty is a remarkable, sometimes moving document. It contains the daily notes of a dying man who gives no indication that he knows what lies before him. Though as pithy as always, a serene cheerfulness speaks through these notes, a state of mind not to be attributed to great intellectual detachment alone.

These last notebooks were Wittgenstein's response to two essays by his predecessor in the Cambridge chair of philosophy, G. E. Moore. In these essays[88] Moore attempts to allay Cartesian doubt about the security of all knowledge claims by giving a whole series of propositions that he can justifiably claim to know with indubitable certainty and for good reasons. These propositions include "I know this is a hand" (expressed while the speaker holds up one of his hands), "I know that the earth existed long before my birth," and other "common-sense" propositions. Indistinguishable in form from ordinary empirical propositions, these propositions are nonetheless, in Moore's view, absolutely certain.

---

87. Compare the notes on conversations in Malcolm's *Memoir,* pp. 70ff.

88. "A Defense of Common Sense" and "Proof of an External World." Cf. von Wright, "Wittgenstein on Certainty."

Wittgenstein was interested both in the idea that the foundations of knowledge might be disclosed by stating contingent, empirical propositions, and in what Moore implied about the use of the word "know." Although he had been concerned with both themes in earlier writings, he expresses himself more pregnantly about the first theme in *On Certainty* than elsewhere. He had said a good deal about the grammar of "know" in *Philosophical Investigations* and *Remarks on the Philosophy of Psychology;* this material both anticipates some of his last remarks and provides them with a more extensive framework.

Many of Wittgenstein's reflections on the concept of knowledge start from the observation that we tend to regard knowing as the highest stage of a hierarchically ordered series of attitudes toward possible objects of knowledge. When we are not sure that something is the case, we can speak of assuming, suspecting, or believing it. When, on the other hand, we are quite sure that something is so, we claim to know it. Thus we say with increasing confidence: "I can't exclude the possibility that an Alpine rose is blooming in his garden"; "I suspect that he stole the car"; "I believe that his son attends the same class as mine"; "I know the book's in the bedroom." In view of this hierarchical arrangement of attitudes based on degrees of confidence (with supposition on the bottom and knowledge on top), we all too easily draw the conclusion that all definitely indubitable propositions are at the same time propositions whose contents are known. From the premise that we cannot doubt for a moment that the book is in the bedroom, we may conclude that we know it is in the bedroom. Maybe so. But what about "If it's in the bedroom, it's in the bedroom," or "1 + 1 = 2"? Can it really be said that one *knows* such things? It puts a strain on the imagination to imagine situations in which such knowledge claims are possible and do not give the impression of being totally inappropriate.

One cannot always speak of knowing when doubt is out of the question. This is a point Wittgenstein explains in detail, especially in connection with statements about states of consciousness. Thus, in section 246 of the *Philo-*

sophical *Investigations,* he has his conversation partner say, in a fully common-sense tone of voice: "Well, only I can know if I'm really in pain; others can only suspect that I am." The dialogue continues:

> [Wittgenstein:] In one way that is incorrect, in another, nonsense. If we use the word "know" as it is normally used (and how else should we use it!), then others very often know when I'm in pain.
>
> [Partner:] Yes, but not with the certainty that I myself know it!
>
> [Wittgenstein:] One cannot say of me (except in jest) that I *know* I'm in pain. What is it supposed to mean—except perhaps that I *am* in pain?

It is precisely because all doubt is out of the question in my own case that Wittgenstein denies that I can assert that I *know* myself to be in pain. Of course, the way doubt is impossible for me here is different from the way it was impossible for me to doubt that the book is in the bedroom. Saying "I *know* the book is there" is the same as saying "There's no doubt in my mind about it." Yet you have the right to respond by asking "Are you sure?" or "Do you really know that?" But when we are talking about my pain, you cannot sensibly respond with "Are you sure you're in pain?" or "Do you really know it?" When I say that I am in pain, I am myself the highest authority. I can neither prove nor doubt whether I am in pain, hungry, or thirsty. Other people can, in such cases, question my honesty, but not my knowledge. For I simply *have* these sensations.

The principle governing these reflections is stated by Wittgenstein as follows:

> One says "I know" where one can also say "I believe" or "I suspect"—where one can make sure. (If you object that one sometimes says things like "I must, after all, know if I'm in pain!" and "Only you can know what you feel," you should think about the occasions and purpose of these ways of talking. "War is war!" is not an example of the law of identity, either.) (*PI,* p. 221).

Accordingly, the use of "know" is meaningful only in those situations in which doubt is not "logically" ruled out—in situations, therefore, in which words such as "believe" and "suspect" are, in principle, permissible. It would be at best comical were I to speak of "suspecting that I'm in pain," or something of the sort.

One can certainly imagine circumstances here in which one could speak of "knowing." Wittgenstein gives these examples: "I, after all, must know if I'm in pain!" and "Only you can know what you feel." But he adds that one has to be clear about the occasions leading to this way of speaking. One does not say "War is war!" in order to express an identity determination, but rather, for example, to remind someone that people behave differently in wartime than in peacetime, and that he must come to terms with that, etc. Similarly, the proposition "I must know if I'm in pain!" may be meant to rebuke someone who kept insisting that I am in pain when, in fact, I am not. And, finally, the proposition "Only you can know what you feel" may be used as a grammatical remark to *reprimand* someone for presuming that we can, or want to, guess his every emotion: "Just tell us how you feel!"

The basis of this train of thought is the conviction that, normally, a statement is sensibly used only when a stronger, weaker, or opposite statement could be made in the same situation. If the opposite (or increasingly stronger/weaker) statement is impossible, then the use of the expression in question is permissible only in very special and unusual circumstances, circumstances that will affect the sense of the statement.

Wittgenstein explains other expressions in the same way—the expression "to make sure of something," for example:

> One can imagine a case in which I *could* make sure that I have two hands. Normally, though, I can*not*. "But you only need to hold them before your eyes."—If *now* I doubt that I have two hands, why should I believe my eyes? (I might as well ask a friend.) (*PI*, p. 221).

This means that a test is possible only when the basis of the test, or the instruments employed in it, are not themselves brought into question. After an accident I can make sure that I still have my hands because there is reason for doubt in that situation. Under normal circumstances, however, neither the doubt nor the making sure are meaningful. If I have doubts *here,* I can no longer depend on anything.

It is important to note that these remarks are concerned to bring out, not remarkable facts, but insights into linguistic relationships. This point comes out in the following passage in which Wittgenstein first formulates his findings "materially," then shifts them onto an explicitly linguistic plane:

> I can know what the other person is thinking, not what I am thinking.
>
> It is correct to say "I know what you're thinking," wrong to say "I know what I'm thinking."
>
> (An entire cloud of philosophy condenses to one droplet of grammar.) (*PI,* p. 222).

Of course, we must bear in mind that these observations are not "purely linguistic" in that they include the context of use of the expressions involved. This becomes clear in the following remark, which refers to an example from Moore:

> That has to do with the fact that the proposition "The earth has existed for millions of years," for instance, has a clearer sense than "The earth has existed for the last five minutes." For, if you asserted the latter, I would ask you: "What observations does this proposition refer to, and what would count against it?"—whereas I am already familiar with the observations and train of thought to which the former proposition belongs. (*PI,* p. 221).

Among other things, Wittgenstein wants to be rid of a certain principle that philosophers are apt to employ, namely the principle that every proposition logically implied by a meaningful proposition is itself meaningful—that is, can be meaningfully expressed, under normal conditions. He wants to show, from a new angle, the extent to which the sense of an expression is connected with the circumstance of its use. I can certainly imagine a whole series of circumstances in which the statement "The earth has exited for millions of years" is meaningful—for instance, when I want to enlighten a child or a savage about such things. Now, "The earth has existed for the last five minutes" certainly follows logically from "The earth has existed for millions of years." But in what circumstances can I meaningfully assert it? Neither the child nor the savage will have the slightest doubt that the earth has existed for the last five minutes. Why, then, should I say it?

There are all sorts of situations in which I can say that I know something: for example, when I am taking a test or instructing others, when (on occasion) I want to show that I am sure of myself. The use of the word "know" is connected in all these contexts with the way other words are used—connected, perhaps, with the series "believe, suspect . . . ," and with the words "doubt," "error," "confidence," "certainty," and others. Important as it is to see these connections, however, it is equally important to guard against being misled by analogies and carried away by the construction of series. The *peculiarity* of Moore's propositions ("This is a hand," "I know that I've never been far from the surface of the earth," etc.) suggests that there is a present danger of being misled. Wittgenstein wants to show how it is brought to light that one has been misled, and how it comes about that one is misled.

What Moore says contains the seeds of error. His view really comes to this:

> . . . the concept "know" is analogous to the concepts "believe,"
> "surmise," "doubt," "be convinced," in that the statement "I
> know . . ." cannot be an error. And if that *is* so, then an
> inference to the truth of an assertion can be drawn from
> such an utterance. And here the possibility of saying "I
> thought I knew" is overlooked. (*OC*, § 21).[89]

---

89. In the following, all paragraph specifications refer to *On Certainty*, unless otherwise indicated.

Here the word "utterance" [*Äußerung*] is used in Wittgenstein's special sense of a direct, noncorrectable utterance. As in the case of "My head hurts" and the like, my utterance is not something that I base on examining myself and applying criteria. If I say "I believe it rained yesterday" or "I believe in the goodness of mankind," no one can counter my statement by proving that it did not rain anywhere in the area yesterday or by giving all kinds of examples of the evils men do. If I believe these things, then I believe them: here I am the highest authority. If someone says that X thinks that it rained yesterday, I can of course object that, as a matter of fact, it did not rain yesterday. And, given that X usually believes only what has been established, I can doubt that X really believes it. But if X himself tells me he believes it, then I have no right at all to doubt it, unless I have reason to think that he lies.

The word "know" usually behaves quite differently, however. Should someone claim to know that Coburg is the capital of the Federal Republic, I can convince him of his error by indicating facts with the help of an encyclopedia, an atlas, and the like, so that he will have to withdraw his claim and replace it with "I *believed* that I knew . . ." (On the other hand, the expressions "believing that I believed" or "believing that I doubted" are normally out of the question.) Herein lies a basic difference between the series "to believe," "to surmise," etc., on the one hand, and the expression "to know," on the other.

When I say "I believe it rained yesterday," error is in a certain way out of the question. I can be wrong about the fact that it rained yesterday; I *cannot* be wrong about the fact that I believe it did. Here error is ruled out "grammatically," by virtue of the language game. An error is something that can be proven. On the other hand, I can no more prove that a statement about my own beliefs is true than I can prove that I made an error about them. The concepts of error and knowledge belong together. Where speakers can lay claim to knowledge, there it is also possible to catch them in error. In addition to belief-statements, there is a whole series of statements that leave no room for error. Moore's statements belong in this series, as do the following from Wittgenstein: "That I am a man rather than a woman can be verified, but if I were to say I am a woman, and wanted to explain the error by saying that I hadn't checked the statement, no one would let the explanation stand" (§ 79). There can actually be no talk at all of error in this case: If I incorrectly thought myself a woman, I could not explain that away by saying that I made an error; rather, people would naturally suspect that I was suffering from a mental disorder.[90] If I think of myself as a woman, and try to be taken for one, there can be a cause for this in the way I was brought up or in my instinctive life. Such things can be ascertained, and perhaps "treated"; however, there can be no longer talk of verifying, falsifying, and correcting opinions. "Can we say that an *error* has a ground as well as a cause?" (§ 74), Wittgenstein asks. The answer, he suggests, is roughly that a person's error can be fitted into what he knows aright.

World Picture

A reason or ground must always be intersubjective; it is never something only *I* can invoke. One can support one's position with reasons in discussions with others, can cite reasons when one wants to persuade. I claim to know that something is the case on the grounds that, definitely, something else is the case. In other words, if I am justified in a knowledge claim, I can give a reason for it. And if someone else justifiably says that I am in error, he can give grounds for saying so. It is not just that knowledge

---

90. "For months I have lived at address A, have read the name of the street and the number of the house countless times, have received countless letters here and given the address to countless people. If I am in error about it, the error is hardly less than if I were (wrongly) to believe I were writing Chinese and not German./ If my friend were to imagine one day that he had been living for a long time past in such and such a place, etc. etc., I would call this not a *error* but a—perhaps transient—mental disturbance. / Not every false belief of this kind is an error" (*OC*, §§ 70-72).

and error belong to the area of the intersubjective; it is, above all, that they belong always to a single context— indeed to a system, more or less. If you say "I know that Bozen is in southern Tirol," you must be able to go on to explain that Bozen is a city, that southern Tirol is in Europe, etc. If you are unable to do that, we will argue that you do not know that Bozen is in southern Tirol, even though it is. If you say "Innsbruck is in southern Tirol" but are unable to fit what you say into a geographical framework, then you cannot be said to have made an error, even though it is false that Innsbruck is in southern Tirol. As it were, no place has been prepared for an error. For only someone with geographical knowledge can make a geographical error, admit and correct a geographical error, etc.

In this respect, Moore's propositions also behave strangely. It is difficult to fit "I have never gone far from the surface of the earth" into a context, nor is it entirely clear what might count as an "error" here. But there is something else remarkable: we normally claim to know something only when presuming that the other person is ignorant of what we are claiming to know. If a friend has been keeping his birth date a secret, I might tell him that I know it's November 11. This might be described as "surprising him with what I know." But I can hardly expect to surprise him in the sense of giving him a piece of unfamiliar news. In the normal case of expressing what one knows, the speaker assumes that what is said is unknown to the listener. But in the case of Moore's propositions, it is of no importance who says them, or to whom they are said. "I have spent my entire life in close proximity to the earth" is not a statement that only I (and perhaps a few others) can justifiably make; here it makes no difference, practically speaking, who the speaker is. For this reason Wittgenstein asks: "Why doesn't Moore mention, for example, knowing that there is a village called so-and-so in such-and-such part of England among the things he knows? In other words, why does he not mention some *fact* known to him but not to *all* of us?" (§ 462). The peculiarity of Moore's propositions is that I can always be "speaking of myself instead of Moore" (§ 93).

Like statements of error, statements of what we know function only within a certain unquestioned context. Such a context is normally provided by the relevant language game. The playing of the language game is imbedded in a context whose existence is disclosed by way of Moore's propositions. That Wittgenstein imputes such a context is already apparent in section 242 of the *Philosophical Investigations,* which says that communication by means of language requires not only agreement as to definitions but also—"strange as this may sound"—agreement in judgments. The question of what constitutes this context is a theme in Wittgenstein's last notebooks, where he introduces the concept of "world picture." The following is one of the most suggestive passages in the whole work:

But I do not have my world picture because I have convinced myself of its correctness, nor because I am convinced of its correctness. Rather, it is the inherited background against which I distinguish between true and false.

The propositions that describe this world picture could belong to a kind of mythology. And their role is similar to that of the rules of a game; and the game can also be learned purely practically, without explicit rules.

One could imagine that certain propositions having the form of empirical propositions were hardened and functioned as channels for the empirical propositions that were not hardened but fluid; and that this relationship changed with time, fluid propositions hardening and hard ones becoming fluid.

The mythology can revert to a state of flux, the river bed of thoughts can shift. But I distinguish the movement of the water in the river bed from the movement of the river bed itself, even though the two are not sharply divided.

But if it were said, "Therefore, logic is itself an empirical science," that would be wrong. What is right is that the same sentence may be treated now as something to test by experience, later as a rule of testing.

Yes, the bank of the river consists partly of hard rock that is subject to no change or to imperceptible change only, partly of sand that is washed away and redeposited, first here then there. (§§ 94-99).

Much in this passage seems to strikingly anticipate Quine's "field of force" or "network" characterization of our conceptual scheme.[91] It is also in many respects reminiscent of Wittgenstein's "Remarks on Frazer's *The Golden Bough*"— as when he says, "an entire mythology is contained in our language" (p. 70). It should be noted, however, that Wittgenstein is not using the word "mythology" in its usual sense. He does not want to say that there is no fundamental difference between a theory based on the gods of Homer and a theory based on Max Plank and Einstein. Rather, his purpose is to stress that, just as with a mythology: (1) our world picture is a system or structure of not easily removed and replaced convictions; (2) our world picture is tied to our practice; (3) our world picture rests on neither empirical knowledge nor verification of hypotheses; (4) our world picture is not easily shaken by conflicting empirical propositions; (5) a changeover to another system would have the character of a conversion. Let us expand these points.

(1) Although the convictions making up our world picture form a system, we should not compare this system to a theory, that is, to a number of propositions based on axioms or hypotheses, and derivable from them. The system is a totality of judgments that do not need to be formally distinguished from everyday propositions. Although these judgments constitute end points of doubt and justification, we do not, in any acceptable sense of the word, presuppose them; although they certainly provide the "final court of appeal" in some language games, they are not themselves thinkable apart from our other judgments and

---

91. Cf. Quine, "Two Dogmas of Empiricism," § 6. In spite of striking parallels, there are, of course, differences between Wittgenstein's theses and the view of the pragmatist Quine. As one might have anticipated, Wittgenstein offered resistance against the pragmatic interpretation: "So I am trying to say something that sounds like pragmatism?/ A kind of weltanschauung is thwarting me here." (*OC*, § 422).

convictions. Where no further doubt is admissible, I have reached "the foundation of my convictions." "And one could almost say of these foundation walls that they are carried by the entire house" (§ 248). The system making up our world picture is not only the rock on which doubts shatter, it is at the same time the framework in which our discussions have support and our proofs can be preserved: "All testing, all confirming and disconfirming of hypotheses takes place within a system. And this system is not a more or less arbitrary and doubtful point of departure for all our arguments; it belongs, rather to the essence of what we call an argument. The system is not so much the point of departure for arguments as it is the element in which they live" (§ 105).

(2) All demonstrations and discussions take place within the common framework of our world picture. The existence and function of this framework are revealed when, in our efforts at justification, we run up against a limit and can only say "This is the way we do it!" "Proof and justification by evidence come to an end;—however, the end is not a kind of *seeing* on our part, i.e., it is not that certain propositions become directly evident to us as true; rather, it is our *action* that lies at the basis of the language game" (§ 204). Because our action provides the highest appeal for our games of proving and justifying, we cannot depend on a simple catalogue of rules, but must introduce examples as well: "In order to establish a practice, rules are not enough; one needs examples as well. Our rules leave the back doors open, and the practice must speak for itself" (§ 139). Since we are not to think of the founding role of the world picture as being analogous to a structure of hypotheses, Wittgenstein quotes Faust: "In the beginning was the deed" (§ 402).

(3) Although many propositions that we would like to employ as final justifications have, as Wittgenstein shows, the form of common empirical propositions, the world picture itself does not rest on an empirical basis. Everything belonging to empirical knowledge can be tested. But testing must come to an end somewhere, and "the end is not an ungrounded assumption, but an ungrounded way of

acting" (§ 110). We run up against the limits of doubting and justifying not only in our statements about the world of experience but also in our scientific, technical, and practical ways of proceeding. Thus, "one cannot conduct experiments if there are not some things one does not doubt—which is not to say, however, that one takes certain assumptions on faith" (§ 337). Excluding further doubts in this activity does not amount to plugging up all possible holes by leaving relevant assumptions unquestioned. It is just that doubts do not arise: "When I am conducting an experiment, I do not doubt the existence of the apparatus in front of me. I have lots of doubts, but not *that* one. When solving a problem in arithmetic, I believe without doubt that the numbers on the paper will not change places on their own; moreover, I continue to trust my memory, and trust it unconditionally" (§ 337).

Our world picture is not based on what we have examined with special care and therefore know with special certainty. Children swallow down the trivialities of their community's world picture along with the material they learn. Learning takes place mainly not by setting up hypotheses and verifying or disproving them, but by simply accepting and assimilating whatever is taught. Learning is based on believing (§ 170), and by "believing" here Wittgenstein does not mean a lower form of knowledge but (above all) a certain attitude on the part of learners to unhesitatingly treat as valid what they are being taught, and to assimilate it. It is important that what is at issue here is an organized and comprehensive structure, rather than a set of isolated or even disconnected judgments. For we are taught *judgments* and their connection with other judgments.

A *totality* of judgments is made plausible to us.

When we begin to *believe* something, we begin to believe an entire system of propositions, not a single proposition. (Light is shed gradually over the whole.)

It's not individual axioms that appear evident to me; it's a system in which conclusions and premises give each other *mutual* support. (§§ 140-42).

(4) Our practice or form of life supports our language games and gives our judgments certainty. Even if others have long since accepted other procedures, we can hold fast to our practices, as long as they continue to function at all. Saying, in the language game, that I know this and that is the same as saying: I am certain about it; I'll stick with it. To say such a thing is to make a kind of *decision* for a certain viewpoint and for what is to count in the game as evidence and proof. A decision is something one can keep to, or take back. As long as I keep to it, I can exclude all uncomfortable assertions and cling to the world picture I've always had—as I would cling to a mythology. Our world picture can coexist with that of another group. Here Wittgenstein recalls the possibility of different mathematical practices. That I can be so sure of my procedures does not mean that others have to proceed as I do, for what is held without doubt within the framework of my system does not necessarily apply to the practice (the language game) of others:

> One must understand here that complete absence of doubt at some point need not falsify a language game, even where we would say that "justifiable" doubts can exist. For there is also something like *another* arithmetic.

> I believe that this confession must be fundamental to all understanding of logic. (§ 375).

Every practical procedure must certainly come to terms with the setting in which it is practiced. So language games involving knowledge and judgments about the world will sooner or later run into hard facts. This is not because of crass theoretical disharmonies; rather, a great many disturbances, and a constant pressure to adapt the old system to apparently recalcitrant facts deprives the language game of its naturalness, and us of our accustomed confidence. And we may in this way be required to change our procedure. (Cf. § 616f.)

(5) If two incompatible world pictures collide, they will do battle, "each declaring the other foolishness and heresy" (§ 611). We would, of course, first try to convince the repre-

sentatives of the other world picture of the falseness of their view by giving *reasons*. But reasons do not go far in this case. "At the end of reasons stands *persuasion*. (Think of what happens when missionaries convert natives.)" (§ 612).

Referring to one of Moore's examples, Wittgenstein imagines the following case of conversion:

> . . . one can ask: "Can someone have a cogent reason for believing that the world has existed for only a short time— only since his own birth, for instance?" Would he have a good reason to doubt it, assuming that he was always told so? People have believed that they could make rain. Why shouldn't a king be raised in the belief that the world began with him? And if Moore and this king got together and talked, could Moore really prove the correctness of his own belief? I am not saying that Moore could not convert the king to his view, but it would be a special kind of conversion: the king would be brought to the point of seeing the world differently. (§ 92).

Reasons are compelling only within a certain language game, and only when the discussants have compatible world pictures. Of course, I might be able to move someone to give up his conception of the world and to accept mine, but if I do, that will not be because I was successful in providing him with reasons that were correct and cogent according to his own ideas. What I can to do is to present my view in such a way that he is convinced—or indeed overwhelmed—by its elegance or practical utility. It is not reasons within my system or his that convert him, but features of the whole system. Thus: ". . . one is sometimes convinced of the *correctness* of a view by its *simplicity* or *symmetry,* i.e., these are what brings one over to this view. Then one simply says something like: '*That's* how it must be' " (§ 92).

The most striking thing about the "shifting river bed" passages is the idea "that certain propositions having the form of empirical propositions were fixed and served as channels for the non-fixed and fluid empirical propositions, and that this relationship changed with time, so that fluid propositions would become fixed, and the fixed would flow again." Wittgenstein makes several attempts to elucidate this idea. In one passage, § 321, he says that every empirical proposition can be "turned into a postulate—thereby becoming a norm of description."⁹² But he is not satisfied with this formulation and says that it reminds him too much of the *Tractatus*—by which he means that it is too general, without sufficient regard for practical possibilities. In sections 308–309 he establishes that "not everything having the form of an empirical proposition is an empirical proposition," wondering whether rule and empirical proposition merge now and then. And in section 401 he writes: "Propositions having the form of empirical propositions, and not propositions of logic alone, belong to the foundation of all operation with ideas (with language)." Yet just two sentences later he notes that the expression "propositions having the form of empirical propositions" is "very bad." What he dislikes about it, he does not make explicit. But he is presumably alluding to the fact that not all empirical propositions share the same "form."

Even though Wittgenstein is not satisfied with his own formulations, the idea he wants to present is clear enough, namely, that everyday propositions about objects of possible experience can change their function in the language game—can lose their descriptive character, becoming norms or rules of the language game. This idea may sound harmless enough, but it is not easy to understand or assimilate. In Quine's related conception, the function of a proposition and its relatively central or peripheral position is judged according to whether it is to a larger or smaller degree

---

92. Cf. *OC*, § 167: "That our empirical propositions do not all have the same status is clear from the fact that one can lay down such a proposition and turn it from an empirical proposition into a norm of description. / Think of chemical investigations. Lavoisier experiments with substances in his laboratory and concludes that this and that takes places when burning occurs. He does not say that it might happen differently another time. He makes use of a definite world picture—not one that he invented, of course, but one that he learned as a child. I say world picture and not hypothesis, because it is the matter-of-course foundation for his research and as such also goes unmentioned."

"formal" or "substantive." Thus, propositions of mathematics or logic have practically no empirical content and are accordingly assigned to the center of the conceptual scheme. The greater a proposition's empirical content, the closer it is to the periphery. This view certainly seems obvious, yet Wittgenstein rejects it. He says expressly that propositions about objects, as well as logical propositions, belong to the foundation.

The propositions of mathematics are "fossils" (§ 657); "as it were, the official stamp of incontestability has been put on them" (§ 655). But a proposition such as "My name is . . ." has to get along without this official stamp: for the speaker in question, however, it is fixed just as incontestably as a mathematical proposition, so it can fulfil its function in a similar way.

Certain everyday (or all-too-everyday) propositions serve as pivots on which other statements in the language game can turn; they have thereby ceased to be suitable in all contexts for fulfilling the tasks of everyday propositions. "Some things seem to us fixed, taken out of circulation. They are shunted onto a side track, so to speak" (§ 210). Moore's propositions seem remarkable because they are like that. If a proposition appears in the guise of everyday language, we expect to be able to make mistakes about it, and expect that the usual game of verification, examination, and confirmation applies to it. But our expectation is unfulfilled in the case of propositions such as "This is a hand," where doubts are out of the question. But then, according to Wittgenstein, we should not really speak of knowing them either. Propositions that preclude doubt and error can point to what provides certainty in playing the language game, but they have lost their everyday function and stand over on a "side track." Such propositions resume participation in normal linguistic intercourse only through a conceptual shift due to a change in our language game— that is, in our life.

Again and again in his final investigations of the concept of certainty, Wittgenstein encounters boundaries, boundaries that (in part) had emerged in earlier writings. He had said: we follow the rule blindly; this language game is played; forms of life are what has to be accepted, the given. Here he says:

> You must consider that the language game is, so to speak, something unpredictable. I mean that it is not based on grounds. [Is] not reasonable (or unreasonable).
>
> It is there—like our life. (§ 559).

That reason cannot go beyond these boundaries is not to say that the investigation ends in the irrational. Our actions do not have to be viewed only through the eyes of the theoretician, however—that is, from the point of view of someone accustomed to stacking proof on proof, interpretation on interpretation:

> Here I want to view the human being as an animal, as a primitive creature credited with instinct but not ratiocination. As a creature in a primitive state. For whatever logic suffices for a primitive means of understanding need not be a source of shame for us either. (§ 475).[93]

Using a very different route, here Wittgenstein has arrived at something similar to what he had found in his early work. "Do I not find myself coming closer and closer to having to say that logic cannot ultimately be described?" Logic can be described here as little as it could in the *Tractatus*. "You must take a look at the practice of language; then you will recognize it" (§ 475). Of course, looking at the practice of language is looking at facts. But it is not

> . . . self-evident that the possibility of a language game is conditioned by certain facts.

---

93. Cf. *RPP*, Vol. II, § 689: "First comes instinct, then reasoning. There are no reasons until there is a language game."

It would seem, then, that the language game would have to "show" the facts that make it possible. (But it does not.) (§§ 617f.).

Here, as in the *Tractatus,* the philosopher can help us to see logic only by seeing to it that logic shows itself. But the *facts* that play a role do not show themselves.

Bibliography

Translators' note: In view of our audience, we have wherever possible cited the English-language editions corresponding to the German-language works cited in Schulte's bibliography. We want to emphasize strongly, as we stated in the preface, that we, not the authors listed in the following bibliography, are responsible for the translations of Wittgenstein's German found in the preceding text. We wanted to provide fresh English versions of the passages quoted by Schulte.

I. Wittgenstein's Writings

Note: As is customary, passages from the *Tractatus* are referred to by the corresponding decimal numbering. The *Philosophical Investigations, Remarks on the Foundations of Mathematics, Remarks on the Philosophy of Psychology,* and *On Certainty* usually are referred to by paragraphs ("§§"). (Only in the case of the *Investigations* does the paragraph numbering originate with Wittgenstein.) Remaining specifications refer to the pages of the respective writing. Abbreviations are provided for commonly cited works.

Main Works

BB *The Blue and Brown Books.* 2d ed. New York: Harper and Row, 1969.

CV *Culture and Value.* Translated by Peter Winch. Chicago: University of Chicago Press, 1980.

LW *Last Writings on the Philosophy of Psychology.* Translated by C. G. Luckhardt and M. A. E. Aue. Chicago: University of Chicago Press, 1982.

NB *Notebooks, 1914–1916* (in reality the notes go to 1917). 2d ed. Translated by G. E. M. Anscombe. Chicago: University of Chicago Press, 1979.

NL "Notes on Logic," in *NB.*

"Notes Dictated to G. E. Moore in Norway," in *NB.*

OC *On Certainty.* Translated by Denis Paul and G. E. M. Anscombe. New York: Harper and Row, 1969.

PG *Philosophical Grammar.* Translated by Anthony Kenny. Berkeley: University of California Press, 1974.

PI *Philosophical Investigations.* 3d ed. Translated by G. E. M. Anscombe. New York: Macmillan, 1958.

PR *Philosophical Remarks.* Translated by Raymond Hargreaves and Roger White. Chicago: University of Chicago Press, 1975.

RC *Remarks on Color.* Translated by Linda L. McAlister and Margarete Schättle. Berkeley: University of California Press, 1977.

RFM *Remarks on the Foundations of Mathematics.* Translated by G. E. M. Anscombe. Rev. ed. Cambridge: MIT Press, 1978.

RPP *Remarks on the Philosophy of Psychology.* 2 vols. Translated by G. E. M. Anscombe (Vol. I) and C. G. Luckhardt and M. A. E. Aue (Vol. II). Chicago: University of Chicago Press, 1980.

TLP *Tractatus Logico-Philosophicus.* Translated by D. F. Pears and B. F. McGuinness. New York: Humanities Press, 1961.

WVC *Wittgenstein and the Vienna Circle.* Conversations recorded by Friedrich Waismann. Translated by Joachim Schulte and Brian McGuinness. New York: Barnes and Noble, 1979.

Z *Zettel.* Translated by G. E. M. Anscombe. Berkeley: University of California Press, 1967.

Further Writings

"Cause and Effect: Intuitive Awareness." *Philosophia* 6 (1976), pp. 391–445.

Prototractatus. An early version of the *TLP.* London: Routledge and Kegan Paul, 1971.

RF "Remarks on Frazer's *The Golden Bough.*" In *Wittgenstein: Sources and Perspectives,* C. G. Luckhardt, ed., pp. 61ff. Ithaca, N.Y.: Cornell University Press.

"Some Remarks on Logical Form," in *Proceedings of the Aristotelian Society,* Supplementary Vol. 9 (1929), pp. 162–71.

"Wittgenstein's Notes for Lectures on 'Private Experience' and 'Sense Data'." In *Introduction to the Philosophy of Mind*, Harold Morick, ed., pp. 152ff. Glenview, Ill.: Scott, Foresmann, and Co., 1970.

Lectures

L&C *Lectures and Conversations on Aesthetics, Psychology and Religious Belief*, compiled by Cyril Barrett from notes of Yorick Smythies, Rush Rhees, and James Taylor. Berkeley: University of California Press, 1966.

LE "A Lecture on Ethics." *Philosophical Review* 74 (1965): pp. 3–12.

LFM *Lectures on the Foundations of Mathematics, Cambridge, 1939*. Compiled by Cora Diamond from notes of R. G. Bosanquet, Norman Malcolm, Rush Rhees, and Yorick Smythies. Ithaca, N.Y.: Cornell University Press, 1976.

ML G. E. Moore, "Wittgenstein's Lectures in 1930–33." In *Philosophical Papers*, G. E. Moore, pp. 252–324. London: Allen and Unwin, 1959.

"The Language of Sense Data and Private Experience," notes of Rush Rhees. In *Philosophical Investigations*, Vol. 7 (1984), pp. 1–45 and pp. 101–40.

WLA *Wittgenstein's Lectures, Cambridge, 1932–1935*, from the notes of Alice Ambrose and Margaret Macdonald. (Edited by Ambrose.) Totowa, N.J.: Rowman and Littlefield, 1979.

WLL *Wittgenstein's Lectures, Cambridge, 1930–1932*, from the notes of John King and Desmond Lee. (Edited by Lee.) Totowa, N.J.: Rowman and Littlefield, 1980.

Letters

Letters from Ludwig Wittgenstein, with a Memoir. Oxford: Blackwell, 1967. (Also contains an important letter from Wittgenstein to L. von Ficker, on pp. 143f.)

Letters to C. K. Ogden. London and Boston: Routledge and Kegan Paul, 1973.

Letters to Russell, Keynes and Moore. New York: Cornell University Press, 1974.

"Letters to von Wright," in *The Cambridge Review,* February 28, 1983.

II. Works Cited

Baker, Gordon, and Peter Hacker. *Meaning and Understanding.* Chicago: University of Chicago Press, 1980.

———. *Skepticism, Rules and Language.* Oxford: Blackwell, 1984.

Black, Max. *A Companion to Wittgenstein's "Tractatus."* Ithaca, N.Y.: Cornell University Press, 1964.

Block, Irving, ed. *Perspectives on the Philosophy of Wittgenstein.* Oxford: Blackwell, 1981.

Bouwsma, O. K. *Wittgenstein, Conversations 1949–1951.* Indianapolis: Hackett, 1986.

Clark, Ronald W. *The Life of Bertrand Russell.* Harmondsworth: Penguin, 1978.

Drury, M. O'C. "Some Notes on Conversations with Wittgenstein" and "Conversations with Wittgenstein." In *Ludwig Wittgenstein: Personal Recollections.* Rush Rhees, ed. Totowa, N.J.: Rowman and Littlefield, 1981.

Englemann, Paul. *Letters from Ludwig Wittgenstein, with a Memoir.* Oxford: Blackwell, 1967.

Fann, K. T., ed. *Ludwig Wittgenstein: The Man and His Philosophy.* New York: Dell, 1967.

Frege, G. *The Foundations of Arithmetic.* Translated by J. L. Austin, 2d edition. Oxford: Blackwell, 1959.

Hacker, Peter. *Insight and Illusion.* Oxford: Oxford University Press, 1972 (rev. 1987).

Haller, Rudolf. "Was Wittgenstein Influenced by Spengler?" In *Questions On Wittgenstein.* Lincoln, Nebr.: University of Nebraska Press, 1988.

Heringer, Hans Jürgen and Michael, eds. *Wittgenstein: Schriften,* Supplementary Vol. 3: *Wittgensteins geistige Erscheinung.* Frankfurt: Suhrkamp, 1979.

Hilbert, David. "Neubegründung der Mathematik." In *Gesammelte Abhandlungen,* Vol. 3. Berlin: J. Springer, 1935.

Hilmy, S. Stephen. *The Later Wittgenstein.* Oxford: Blackwell, 1987.

Hintikka, Merrill B., and Jaakko. *Investigating Wittgenstein.* Oxford: Blackwell, 1986.

Ishiguro, Hidé. "Use and Reference of Names." In Winch, ed., *Studies in the Philosophy of Wittgenstein.*

Janik, Allan, and Stephen Toulmin. *Wittgenstein's Vienna.* New York: Simon and Schuster, 1973.

Kenny, Anthony. "From the Big Typescript to the *Philosophical Grammar.*" In *Acta Philosophica Fennica: Essays on Wittgenstein in Honour of G. H. von Wright,* pp. 41–53. Amsterdam: North Holland, 1976. (Also contained in Kenny's *The Legacy of Wittgenstein,* pp. 24–37. Oxford: Blackwell, 1984).

———. "Wittgenstein on the Nature of Philosophy." in Kenny, *The Legacy of Wittgenstein,* pp. 38–60.

King, John. "Recollections of Wittgenstein." In *Ludwig Wittgenstein: Personal Recollections,* Rhees, ed., pp. 83–90.

Kripke, Saul. *Naming and Necessity.* Cambridge: Harvard University Press, 1972.

———. *Wittgenstein on Rules and Private Language.* Cambridge: Harvard University Press, 1982.

Leavis, F. R. "Memories of Wittgenstein." In *Ludwig Wittgenstein: Personal Recollections,* Rhees, ed., pp. 63–82.

Malcolm, Norman. *Ludwig Wittgenstein: A Memoir.* 2d ed. Oxford: Oxford University Press, 1984.

———. *Nothing is Hidden.* Oxford: Blackwell, 1986.

Mays, Wolfe. "Recollections of Wittgenstein." In *Ludwig Wittgenstein: The Man and His Works,* K. T. Fann, ed.

McGuinness, Brian. *Wittgenstein: A Life. Young Ludwig 1889–1921.* Berkeley: University of California Press, 1988.

———. "The Mysticism of Wittgenstein's *Tractatus.*" *Philosophical Review,* 75 (1966): pp. 305–28.

———. "The So-Called Realism of Wittgenstein's *Tractatus.*" In *Perspectives on the Philosophy of Wittgenstein,* Block, ed., pp. 60–73.

Moore, G. E. "A Defense of Common Sense" (1925) and "Proof of an External World" (1939). Both in *Philosophical Papers,* G. E. Moore. London: Allen and Unwin, 1959.

Pascal, Fania. "Wittgenstein: A Personal Memoir." In *Ludwig Wittgenstein: Personal Recollections,* Rhees, ed., pp. 26–62.

Pears, David. *The False Prison* two volumes. Oxford: Oxford University Press, 1987–88.

———. "The Relation Between Wittgenstein's Picture Theory of Propositions and Russell's Theories of Judgment." *Philosophical Review* 86 (1977): pp. 177–96.

Quine, Willard Van Orman. "Two Dogmas of Empiricism." In *From a Logical Point of View,* pp. 20–46. Cambridge: Harvard University Press, 1961.

Rhees, Rush, ed. *Ludwig Wittgenstein: Personal Recollections.* Totowa, N.J.: Rowman and Littlefield, 1981.

———. "Postscript." In *Ludwig Wittgenstein: Personal Recollections,* Rhees, ed., pp. 190–231.

Russell, Bertrand. *The Theory of Knowledge* (the 1913 manuscript). London: Allen and Unwin, 1984.

Savigny, Eike von. "Seelische Sachverhalte sind von der sozialen Einbettung abhängig: Eine durchgängige Interpretation der *Philosophischen Untersuchungen.*" In *Proceedings of the Tenth International Wittgenstein Symposium* (1985), pp. 461–71. Vienna: Hölder-Pichler-Tempsky, 1986.

Schulte, Joachim. *Erlebnis und Ausdruck. Wittgensteins Philosophie der Psychologie.* Munich: Philosophia, 1987.

———. "Chor und Gesetz. Zur 'morphologischen Methode' bei Goethe und Wittgenstein." In *Grazer philosophische Studien,* Vol. 21 (1984), pp. 1–32.

Strawson, Peter F. "Wittgenstein's *Philosophical Investigations*" (1954). In *Freedom and Resentment and Other Essays,* Strawson, pp. 133–68. London: Methuen, 1974.

Waismann, Friedrich. *The Principles of Linguistic Philosophy.* New York: St. Martin's Press, 1965.

———. *Lectures on the Philosophy of Mathematics.* Amsterdam: Rodopi, 1982.

Winch, Peter. *Trying to Make Sense.* Oxford: Blackwell, 1987.

———. "Language, Thought and World in Wittgenstein's *Tractatus.*" In *Trying to Make Sense,* Winch, pp. 3–17.

———, ed., *Studies in the Philosophy of Wittgenstein.* New York: Humanities Press, 1969.

Wittgenstein, Hermine. "My Brother Ludwig." In *Ludwig Wittgenstein: Personal Recollections,* Rhees, ed., pp. 1–13.

Wittgenstein, Karl. *Politico-Economic Writings.* Amsterdam/Philadelphia: Benjamins, 1984.

Wright, Georg Henrik von. *Wittgenstein.* Minneapolis: University of Minnesota Press, n.d.

———. "Ludwig Wittgenstein: A Biographical Sketch." In *Wittgenstein,* von Wright, pp. 13–34. Also in Malcolm's *Memoir,* pp. 1–20.

———. "The Wittgenstein Papers." In *Wittgenstein,* von Wright, pp. 35–62.

———. "The Origin of the *Tractatus.*" In *Wittgenstein,* von Wright, pp. 63–109.

———. "The Origin and Composition of the *Philosophical Investigations.*" In *Wittgenstein,* von Wright, pp. 111–36.

———. "Wittgenstein on Certainty." In *Wittgenstein,* von Wright, pp. 163–82.

Wünsche, Konrad. *Der Volksschullehrer Ludwig Wittgenstein.* Frankfurt: Suhrkamp, 1985.

Index